BERLIN:
THE EAGLE AND THE BEAR

Frederick William, 'The Great Elector' (1640–1688): founder of modern Prussia
Statue by Andreas Schlüter.

BERLIN:
THE EAGLE AND THE BEAR

BY

JOHN MANDER

LONDON
BARRIE AND ROCKLIFF

FIRST PUBLISHED 1959
BY BARRIE AND ROCKCLIFF (BARRIE BOOKS LIMITED)
2 CLEMENT'S INN, LONDON WC2

PRINTED IN GREAT BRITAIN BY
WESTERN PRINTING SERVICES LIMITED
BRISTOL

CONTENTS

ILLUSTRATIONS

PREFACE

I HAVE attempted in this book to evoke something of the past of a great city. This by its nature is a difficult, even presumptuous undertaking, and it should be said at once that *The Eagle and the Bear* does not purport to be a history of Berlin. This book ignores the medieval and renaissance periods almost completely, on the grounds that they are less specifically '*berlinisch*' than the period that begins with the accession of the Great Elector in 1640. They are also, I think, unlikely to interest the English or American reader.

For similar reasons I have preferred a somewhat loose chronology. Events, such as the First World War, which have been treated very fully elsewhere and are well known to the average reader are dealt with in what may appear a rather summary fashion. By contrast, literary and artistic movements which are only gradually becoming known outside Germany —*Biedermeier* or the Expressionism of the Twenties—have been treated at considerable length. Many of the personalities described in the book are not, of course, in the strict sense Berliners. Neither Bismarck nor Ernst Reuter, nor for that matter E. T. A. Hoffmann or Bertolt Brecht, can claim to be Berliners by birth. It is enough for the purposes of this book that their main work was done in Berlin and that they became part of its intellectual, political, or literary tradition.

Any lack of balance found in the book, too much literature, too little economics, is likely to be due to the interests and prejudices of the author. A book of this kind cannot be more than an evocation and an evocation is necessarily a subjective thing: a different writer would have written a different book. The present writer can only hope that those who see Berlin through his eyes will feel that they have seen it reasonably straight and whole.

THE HOUSE OF HOHENZOLLERN FROM THE GREAT ELECTOR TO THE LAST KAISER

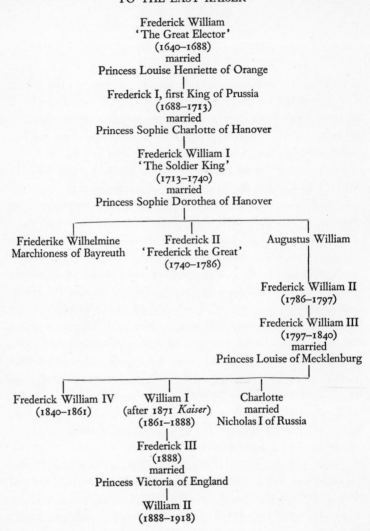

Frederick William
'The Great Elector'
(1640–1688)
married
Princess Louise Henriette of Orange

Frederick I, first King of Prussia
(1688–1713)
married
Princess Sophie Charlotte of Hanover

Frederick William I
'The Soldier King'
(1713–1740)
married
Princess Sophie Dorothea of Hanover

Friederike Wilhelmine
Marchioness of Bayreuth

Frederick II
'Frederick the Great'
(1740–1786)

Augustus William

Frederick William II
(1786–1797)

Frederick William III
(1797–1840)
married
Princess Louise of Mecklenburg

Frederick William IV
(1840–1861)

William I
(after 1871 *Kaiser*)
(1861–1888)

Charlotte
married
Nicholas I of Russia

Frederick III
(1888)
married
Princess Victoria of England

William II
(1888–1918)

Chapter 1

THE EAGLE AND THE BEAR

BERLIN, in 1959, is still a city of ruins. But they are not ruins in which an archaeologist would find much satisfaction. The 'historical remains' of Berlin can be numbered on the fingers of one hand. There are two medieval churches in the centre of the old city: the bombed Nicolaikirche and the restored Marienkirche. There is a fragment of old city wall that came to light after an air-raid; and nearby a little seventeenth-century toll-house. There is the late seventeenth-century Armoury on Unter den Linden with Schlüter's sculptured Heads of Dying Warriors, and, also on Unter den Linden, Frederick the Great's opera house and the palace of his brother Prince Henry, now the Humboldt University. But that is all that is left; and these 'historical remains' are in the Eastern part of the city. Berlin's architecture is otherwise late nineteenth- or early twentieth-century. She is, though the Berliners hotly deny it, almost certainly the ugliest capital city in Europe.

Her attractions must be sought elsewhere: not in visible remains but in history, literature and philosophy. Above all, as we shall try to show in this book, in her history. For, in its way, the ruined landscape of Berlin is as impressive as some jungle-smothered city in Mexico or Cambodia. Pity and terror can seize the observer of this panorama of destruction as he wanders down the wrecked Wilhelmstrasse with his

B   1

Trevor-Roper as he might with Baedecker through the Forum Romanum. The Wilhelmstrasse of the newspaper headlines has vanished utterly; it is no longer the seat of any government and is itself in ruins. Yet its wreck still inspires the visitor with awe, more than a decade after the suicide of the Great Dictator.

From the road it is still possible to make out the two monstrous upturned megaliths which are all that remain of Hitler's *Führerbunker*. The Chancellery itself, in the garden of which it was constructed, is no longer to be found. It has suffered the fate of Carthage and been put—literally—under the plough. Only a few years back it was still possible (though risky, for the area is on the fringe of the Communist Empire and patrolled by People's Police) to clamber over the chunks of reinforced concrete and jungle of fireweed and thistle. It was not difficult to reconstruct the macabre final act in the garden of the Chancellery: the hasty carrying-out of the bodies of the *Führer* and his mistress and their unceremonious disposal in a shell-crater (the Russians now only a few streets away and what was left of the Government's buildings under constant fire). Then the roar and splutter of flames leaping from the ground as the petrol-soaked bodies catch and are quickly consumed, except for some charred remains that the Russians find and remove to an unknown destination. It is Hitler's longed-for *Götterdämmerung*, himself a Siegfried betrayed by his countrymen yet, in his ride into the flames with Brunhilde, one of the Immortals, the master and not the slave of Fate.

It is a barbaric scene and disturbing in more than one way. Should we take it as high tragedy or melodramatic farce? Friedrich Meinecke, the last of the great line of Prussian historians, remarked to a friend who was later executed after the 20th of July bomb plot: 'Hitler is not one of us. He comes of some race we'd long considered extinct.' It was the remark of a Prussian, of a German to whom the sinister pseudo-Faustian Romantic element in his fellow-countrymen had always been a source of alarm and misgiving. We shall try to show that Prussianism was in many ways the counterpart of Romanticism. This is not to say that Berlin represented the Prussian pole in the German character and some other city the Romantic. It is more complex than that. There were oscillations between the poles and strange reversals. There were Prussian Romantics (Ludwig Tieck, Heinrich von Kleist, E. T. A. Hoffmann), and Romantic Prussians (King Frederick William IV, and the last *Kaiser*). But Meinecke was right in thinking that he and his fellow Prussians came of a different race from Adolf Hitler.

The symbol of Prussia was the Eagle, the Eagle of the Hohenzollerns who ruled over Berlin, first as Electors, then as Kings, and finally as *Kaisers*. But before we consider how Prussia and Berlin evolved as they did we must go back to the origins. An idea of Berlin in its beginnings can be obtained easily enough. It is only necessary to drive out into the countryside (Soviet visa required!) and take a look at the March of Brandenburg with its innumerable lakes and forests and flat, sandy roads. This is more or less how Berlin must have looked in the earliest days. Yet the March of Brandenburg is not a monotonous landscape. Before the war it was possible to canoe for hours through its labyrinth of wood and water and enjoy the quite peculiar charm of its blend of conifer and silver-birch. In earlier times oaks would have been predominant, but conifers were found more suited to the sandy soil. It is a very gentle landscape: there is nothing in it of the shuddering pines and gaping chasms of High Romanticism. Only in one respect is the March extreme: in the Baltic winters and biting east winds which it shares with Poland and Russia. Yet, like the Russian climate itself, it is dry and bracing. And it has often been suggested that the Prussians owed their vigour to this combination. Perhaps that is why they chose Berlin as their capital. She may be no beauty, but she can claim the healthiest climate of any city in Europe.

The landscape of Prussia is one of Professor Toynbee's

favourite illustrations of his doctrine of 'challenge and response'. The meagre soil, fit only for growing potatoes, was capable of breeding the finest soldiers and administrators in Europe: Necker, for example, was of Pomeranian stock. 'Challenge and response' may not be the only explanation. One suspects that examples could be found of indolent peoples living in similar landscapes, like the Slav Wends who inhabited the March in the Dark Ages, content to eke out a living as fishermen and trappers. But the poverty of the March certainly moulded the tough virtues of the *Junkers* and their peasants. And is it fanciful to derive the characteristics of the modern Berliner from his ancestors in the March of Brandenburg? Do not his hard-work-and-no-nonsense attitude to life, his cockney humour, and his resourcefulness reflect the life of the pioneers, the first German immigrants of the twelfth century? It is as if the meagreness of the soil had left its mark on the inhabitants of the March: a certain hardness and leanness of body and mind, a thrift extending into everyday speech (the land is *karg*, the people *wortkarg*). The Marchman learned modesty in the face of a nature so inhospitable and ungenerous; a certain irony at the fragility of human achievement became traditional.

But the grittiness of the Marchman is only one element in the constitution of the Berliner. For the Berliner is in reality of very mixed racial stock. The foundation may be German, probably Lower Saxon, but Slav and Latin as well as the other German tribes have contributed to the final product. On a single doorway in present-day Berlin one may find the nameplates of Dr. Kowalski, dentist; Dr. Duval, solicitor; and Dr. Schulze, family doctor and general practitioner. The Kowalskis may have come to Berlin in the middle of the last century as Polish Catholic peasants looking for work in the Prussian capital. The Duvals may be descended from Huguenots who had to leave France when Louis Quatorze revoked the Edict of Nantes. The Schulzes' origin is anybody's guess. They may have come to Berlin from Silesia or the Rhineland or Pomerania. They may have come to seek their fortunes in the army of Frederick the Great or in the new factories of Siemens and Borsig in the 1840's. But the Kowalskis, Duvals and Schulzes have one thing in common. If asked about their ancestry they will almost certainly shrug their shoulders and excuse themselves with pressure of business. The Berliners have not much use for or interest in the past.

Perhaps the Berliners show a sound instinct in this respect. While the rest of Europe is burdened with the fears and anxieties of her past, Berlin has the chance to break with traditional obsessions and build anew. Whether she will be allowed to do so is another question. Her position is at the moment precarious, though not much more so, as we shall see, than at certain other periods in her history. But if she is allowed to build a new life—whether as a Free City or as the capital of a United Germany—her chief asset will necessarily be the Berliners themselves. These have been shaped by their history into a people very different from, say, the Bavarians or the Rhinelanders. They are not always well liked by their compatriots: the Berliners' *Schnauze* (sharp tongue) and their *Schnoddrigkeit* ('lip') offend other Germans who retreat before them into their native *Gemütlichkeit*. The Berliners are no respecters of persons. They are both thick-skinned and a little sentimental, and they expect unreasonably to be loved for their faults. It is perhaps not inappropriate that the ancient mascot and symbol of the city should be a Bear.

Chapter 2

THE BIRTH OF PRUSSIA

1237–1740

IT would be convenient if the emblem of the Bear could be derived from that Albert the Bear who conquered and settled the March in the twelfth century. But the early history of Berlin is obscure. Though the foundation of the city is usually dated from the granting of a charter in 1237, the existence of a town on this spot is mentioned as early as 1106. The Eagle and the Bear are to be found on the earliest town seals. Right from the start Berlin had a double nature, a peculiar ambiguity. Many of the great cities of Germany were free cities of the Empire, free vassals of the Emperor like Frankfurt, Augsburg, Nuremberg, or Hanseatic towns like Bremen, Hamburg or Lübeck; and these latter cities remained politically autonomous up to the time of Bismarck. But Berlin never enjoyed these liberties. It was her fate to have to live for centuries under the shadow of the Eagle, the Hohenzollern eagle or that of the Second and Third *Reich*. But it would be wrong to suppose that because the Berliners rose to Ernst Reuter's challenge to the Soviet colossus with such spirit, their attitude to authority had been one of unambiguous resistance.

Ernst Reuter created a myth in this respect to which, one hopes, the Berliners will be able to live up in the future. Yet it is a myth based on only one element in Berlin's temperament and tradition. The Berliners and their cousins of the March were, after all, the inhabitants of a border province and, in Europe, a strong authority is needed to assure survival under such conditions. In America it was different. There, a young nation expanded in a vacuum. The frontiers were pushed forward by pioneers whose rugged individualist spirit is—if we can believe the Voice of America—still the driving force behind the American way of life. But in overcrowded Europe, above all in Germany with its lack of natural frontiers, Order has often been a matter of life and death, and freedom has often enough been equated with Anarchy. Even as late as the thirteenth century, Mongolian hordes could devastate Hungary and Silesia. And, in German eyes, the barbarian threat to Europe's Eastern frontier has always been over the horizon. Thus for the inhabitants of Berlin the Eagle had, as for other Germans, a double face. It was at once the symbol of despotism at home and of protection against the fury of the world outside. The Anglo-Saxon antinomy of liberty and authority can seem crude to peoples living in more dangerous circumstances. For those without fixed frontiers Authority can seem the guarantor of Liberty.

Yet when the March was bought by the first Hohenzollern, a Burgrave of Nuremberg, in 1411, the new ruler did not come easily into his estate. 'And should it rain Burgraves from Heaven for the space of a whole year, yet shall they not take root in this March of Brandenburg', a dour *Junker* commented who did not care to see so much authority in a prince's hand. The Berliners thought likewise and refused the oath of allegiance, refused even to open the gates of the city to the unknown Hohenzollern. But the Hohenzollerns had the stuff of future kings in them. Frederick I did not hesitate to use his cannon against the *Junkers'* castles and to bring his surly Berliners to reason.

Yet only a few years later his son, Frederick II, was confronted again with the bearishness of the Berliners. They shut the gates of the town in his face as he rode in from Spandau to take formal possession of his inheritance. This second Hohenzollern ordered the town to be stormed, took away its privileges, and built himself a powerful citadel within the town walls, the site of the later Schloss. From that time, it is said, the Bear on the city's coat-of-arms which had previously stood proudly on his hind legs had to go on all fours and, worse still, bear the Hohenzollern Eagle on its broad back. The new rulers had triumphed. Their eagles were to fly over the Schloss from that day in 1486 when the town became the official residence, until those hectic days of November 1918 when the five-hundred-year-old state of the Hohenzollerns was dismantled overnight. It must have seemed in 1918 as if the Bear's chance had come at last.

In fact, as we know, the victory was short-lived. Within fifteen years the Eagle had returned, this time in a far more savage and oppressive form. Yet it is said that Berlin was the one city in Germany of which the Nazis never felt sure; and certainly the quick wit of the Berliners never ceased to mock at the antics of the Nazi bosses. The resistance against Hitler, particularly of the men involved in the 20th of July bomb plot, was to a great extent a Berlin affair. The revolt against the East German regime on the 17th of June 1953 started in Berlin and spread from there over the entire Soviet zone.

Such is the Bear's record of resistance to power in recent decades. It is a good one; but it is not the whole story. The Bear has developed quite a nose for tyranny in his battles with the Eagle; but his attention is easily distracted and he is perhaps more easily taken in than his opposite number in Paris or London. The Berliners were said to be '*militärtoll*', military-mad, before the First World War when even the poorest would flock to the Tempelhof field (now the airport) to watch the trooping of the colours. Many a middle-aged Berliner will admit, somewhat shamefacedly, that the 1936 Olympic Games which the Nazis exploited so skilfully to their own glory was the great event of his life. If the Bear can show his claws, he can also become the victim of his own good humour.

Another element in the Bear's make-up might be mentioned at this point: an extremely stubborn sense of justice. The Berliners were never a religious people; there must be fewer churches in Berlin than in any other city of corresponding size. Yet every Berliner has in him something of that fanatic for righteousness, the legendary Michael Kohlhaas. Kohlhaas, known to German literature as the hero of one of Heinrich von Kleist's stories, was one of the most colourful and bizarre characters thrown up by the German Reformation. These were the years when the Black Death swept over Europe decimating the towns; the times of the great pogroms against Jewry as the scapegoat for these natural disasters. The infamous Tetzel was wandering the length and breadth of Germany trading his indulgences, against which practice Luther nailed his ninety-five theses to the door of Wittenberg Schlosskirche. Many secular rulers had forbidden Tetzel their territory, fearing loss of revenue. The unwary Elector of Brandenburg, however, let him come to Berlin, and Berlin welcomed him as if he were the papal nuncio himself. The town was not rid of him till he had extracted the last *groschen* of conscience-money from the godfearing burghers.

If Tetzel represented medieval Catholicism in its extremities, Kohlhaas was the new Protestant fanatic. His trade was horse-dealing, a trade, as one chronicler remarks, 'with no high reputation for honesty'; and it was on a journey to the horse fair at Leipzig that a Saxon *Junker* relieved him of his two best animals. Kohlhaas appealed to the Elector of Saxony; but the law afforded him no justice. He therefore determined to win justice himself at any cost, even at the cost of reducing wife and children to penury. He organized raiding parties from the safety of the March to plunder not only the *Junker*'s castle but also the lands of the unjust Elector of Saxony. The

Junker took refuge in Wittenberg; whereupon Kohlhaas stormed the town and burnt part of it to the ground. But the Elector had a last resort. He begged Martin Luther to speak to the man and assuage his horrifying thirst for justice. This Luther did. Kohlhaas meekly received the Eucharist from his hand and a promise that the Elector would make good the wrong done to Kohlhaas if the latter would desist from his raiding. With this Kohlhaas returned to Berlin. But the Elector of Saxony failed to keep his promise. Kohlhaas gathered his followers again and threw himself on Saxony in a fury of righteousness. This time, however, the Elector of Brandenburg decided that Kohlhaas had gone too far and gave orders for his arrest. Yet, as Martin Luther had stood against the powers of the world at Worms, so Kohlhaas too would stand up for his rights, if necessary against all the Electors of Germany. He seized a wagon-load of Electoral bullion on its way to Berlin and sank it under a bridge. He was an honest man and had no wish to enrich himself at the Elector's expense: he wished only for justice. (Kohlhaasenbrück still exists, it is the last bus-stop south of the Wannsee before the Soviet zone frontier.) But even a righteous man cannot take up the sword with impunity. Kohlhaas was tricked into returning to Berlin, where he was captured and publicly executed.

The story is something of a parable. For, however the forces released by Luther might seethe and bubble in Germany, it was the princes who had the last word. Lutherans and Calvinists and innumerable smaller sects might squabble for supremacy in the religious life of Berlin, but in the end it was the secular will of the Electors that was supreme. The emblem of a bear on all fours with an eagle on its back was of more than symbolic significance. For the greater part of Berlin's history the Eagle is in the ascendant and the history of the city the history of its ruling dynasty. Not until the years preceding the revolution of 1848 does the Bear really speak with a voice of his own and begin to determine the future of his city.

What, then, of the Hohenzollerns, the ruling dynasty of Prussia? Is there any feature to mark them out from the other petty princes of Germany or from their erstwhile overlords and later rivals, the Habsburgs? Such differences as there are must be due to the environment of the March and its special problems. For, like the Habsburgs, they came from the south-western corner of the *Reich*. The Hohenzollerns were in fact, like the majority of their subjects, immigrants from other parts of Germany. The Prussians were by origin 'colonials', and this is the key to a great deal in their history and that of Berlin. Here the comparison with Habsburg Austria is instructive. Hugo von Hofmannsthal, last and perhaps greatest of her poets, once made a list of the differences in mentality between the two states:

PRUSSIA	AUSTRIA
constructed, an artificial edifice	organic growth, historical plexus
naturally poor country	naturally rich country
everything in Man and for Man	everything from outside, from Nature or God
thus: the State as the basis of unity	love of country as basis of unity
greater virtue	greater piety
greater competence	greater humanity

and between the Prussians and Austrians:

lack of historical sense	historical instinct
gift for abstraction	little gift for abstraction
gift for dialectics	rejection of dialectics

greater consistency	greater adaptability in life
self-confidence	self-irony
apparently masculine	apparently immature
self-righteous, arrogant, schoolmasterly	bashful, vain, witty
thrive on crises	run away from crises
inability to identify themselves with others	identification with others to the detriment of their own personality
character-formation	play-acting
ambition	love of pleasure
primacy of public life	primacy of private life

Interestingly enough the 'Anglo-Saxon attitudes' are disposed fairly evenly on the two sides of the balance. The Austrians had the sense of humour, but the Prussians the stiff upper lip; the Viennese had the social graces, but the Berliners the more solid and humdrum virtues. Yet such speculation is invidious; it is better to study the growth of a culture than to number its virtues and vices. We have suggested that the Prussian qualities of hard-living and plain-thinking were the product of life in the March of Brandenburg. But to complete the synthesis another element was required: the Prussian state. This state, however, had first to be created and its authority made felt in terms of the personal authority of the feudal over-lord. And the Hohenzollerns provided Prussia with three rulers of genius: Frederick William, 'the Great Elector' [1640–1688]; King Frederick William I, known as the 'Soldier King' [1713–1740]; and his son, Frederick II [1740–1786], better known as 'Frederick the Great'.

Frederick William became Elector of Brandenburg in 1640, when the Thirty Years War was in its final decade. The Thirty Years War is to us an episode offstage, but to the Germans it was long the national trauma, the nightmare to which a people returns in its sleep and with which it can never come to terms. We have something similar in the war of King and Parliament; but that conflict was not fought out with the full fury and hatred of the Continental struggle between Protestant and Catholic. Before the end of it many were questioning whether it was not a religious struggle at all but rather a struggle between Powers and Principalities for extremely worldly interests. A similar scepticism in England had helped to give birth to the Royal Society; religious truth being despaired of, men turned to science and the experimental method for enlightenment. In Germany, there were many and varied reactions to that generation of slaughter: ranging from the religious revival of Pietism and the philosophy of Leibniz to the whole panorama of baroque poetry, architecture and music. A no less interesting product of these terrible years is the document known as *The Political Testament of the Great Elector* [1667].

This document is one of the most remarkable ever composed by a reigning monarch, remarkable above all for the utter realism, the pitiless clarity with which he wrote down for his successors the political facts of life. 'Alliances are well enough,' he remarks, 'but one's own forces still better since they are more to be relied upon. A ruler is of no consideration if he does not have adequate means and forces of his own; that alone has made me—thank God for it—a force to be reckoned with. I shall ever regret that at the beginning of my government I was persuaded, to my great disadvantage, to follow any other advice than this.'

The young ruler had seen his country at the mercy first of the Swedish forces and then of those of the Emperor in Vienna. Berlin had been bombarded, the March devastated, and no hurried switching of alliances had been able to save his father's position. The world, it was evident, respected one thing alone: political power based on military strength. A strong army alone can make a ruler 'a force to be reckoned with'; and the Great Elector knew that without it Brandenburg must always be a pawn in the struggles of the great powers. It is the basic proposition of that *Realpolitik* of which Frederick the Great and Bismarck were to be the great exponents.

Realpolitik is a word with an unpleasant flavour. Propaganda would have us believe in a kind of demonic succession from the Great Elector and Frederick the Great through Bismarck and Moltke to Adolf Hitler. But in one respect this hypothesis is certainly false. Hitler was fundamentally a political Idealist and a Romantic, a type not at all uncommon in Germany. Prussia represented quite another pole in the German tradition, a striving for clarity and order, for the classical virtues of objectivity and *mésure*. The Prussian style is that of Moltke's letters and dispatches: economical, well-observed, intellectually agile, and yet matter-of-fact to the point of dryness. It is the impersonal, lean, measured style of Heinrich von Kleist, Prussia's greatest writer, and the style of Schinkel's neo-classical buildings on the Unter den Linden. The Prussian aimed at self-effacement; the Romantic at self-expression.

The great men of German history tend to be of the second type: Luther, Wallenstein, Beethoven, Nietzsche—even Goethe, the anti-Romantic, who described all his works as part of one great confession. But the Prussian, valuing discipline and order above all else, eschewed such eruptions from the depths —and indeed shared something of the English fear of the life of the emotions.

It is a common complaint that in the Prussian view of things freedom was sacrificed to the goddess of Order. But a modern apologist might point out that the ideals of classical Prussia are not to be so lightly dismissed; least of all by modern

Existentialist philosophies that exalt individual responsibility. And, of course, the Prussians could appeal for support to a greater philosophy than Existentialism, to their own Immanuel Kant of Königsberg with his postulates of Freedom, God and Immortality. Plato may have worshipped Sparta from afar; Prussia, the self-designated Sparta of the North, could claim Kant not only as her citizen but as the vindicator of her way of life—a way of life that Englishmen were once brought up to believe a small advance upon savagery.

A Prussian *Apologia* has still to be written (though, as we shall see, Heinrich von Kleist came near to writing it in his *Prince of Homburg*). But it is clear that Hitler did not belong among these self-effacing civil servants and quietly efficient generals, these born administrators who cherished Moltke's motto: '*mehr sein als scheinen*', 'Be rather than Seem'. Hitler was of a different stock; and his political ideas were not part of the Prussian inheritance. Hitler was a political dreamer like the medieval *Kaisers* and like the German Romantics: he had his visions of a Thousand Years' *Reich*. He drew his inspiration not from the Hohenzollern political testaments but from Wagner, Beethoven, and Carlyle, and from those 'infallible intuitions' which caused his Prussian-trained generals to splutter with rage. And whatever Hitler may have practised it was not *Realpolitik*, that unemotional calculation of the real political forces at work in every concrete situation that gave Bismarck his mastery. Thanks to Adolf Hitler the achievements of Prussia over the centuries, built up with such infinite patience and self-denial, were to disappear from the map of Europe overnight. Those who call themselves Prussians by choice—and there are many Berliners who are still proud to do so—were among the bitterest opponents of Nazism. And there were, as we shall see, many Prussians among the men of the 20th of July plot.

But there was a time—forgotten in 1914—when the heroic little Prussia of Frederick the Great, surrounded by more powerful enemies, very much engaged British sympathies. At the Congress of Vienna too, Prussia was still England's Continental favourite; even in 1870 there were divided feelings. It was only after the Franco-Prussian war, when it became apparent that Prussia had made herself top-nation in Europe, that the latter-day Anglo-Saxon notion of her as the root of all evil arose. And it was with feelings of righteous indignation that the Anglo-Saxons signed the death-warrant of Prussia in 1946. The Russian and French signatories of that document may be supposed to have had other motives.

For, in French eyes, Prussia had usurped the French right to hegemony in Europe. The Brandenburger Tor and the Column of Victory in the Tiergarten were a standing insult to *la gloire française;* the former erected in the later eighteenth century, the latter after the Prussian triumph of 1870. The Guards who had once marched with such splendour through the Brandenburger Tor seemed to be marching westwards along the road that leads over the North German plain to the Rhine, the Meuse and the Marne. Yet France and Prussia had not always been cat-and-dog. In the sixteenth, seventeenth, and early eighteenth centuries there had been the traditional alliance of France with the Protestant North German princes against the house of Habsburg; later there were the intellectual ties between Enlightenment and *Aufklärung*; Voltaire, de la Mettrie, La Grange all lived and worked in Berlin. The French derive their picture of German Romanticism from the *grotesqueries* of the Berlin *Kammergerichtsrat* E. T. A. Hoffmann. The Great Elector had offered asylum to tens of thousands of Huguenot exiles, no doubt to the chagrin of Louis Quatorze; and such writers as de la Motte-Fouqué, Fontane, and Lagarde were among their descendants. The spoken language survived into the nineteenth century; and the French lycée founded for the children of these exiles but later patronized by well-to-do families in Berlin has lasted until the present day, when children of French occupation officials and Berlin children sit side by side, all instruction being given in French. But the cat-and-doggery of 1813, 1870, 1914, and 1940 had to come full circle; and at the Potsdam Conference the French saw to it that the accounts were settled. *Delenda est Prussia!*

The old city of Berlin, then, had a westward orientation. But if Prussia had her face turned towards the west, it was because she had her back against a solid wall. And that wall was Russia. The ancient frontier in the north between East Prussia and Russia had existed almost unchanged from the time when the Teutonic Knights converted the heathen 'Borussians' in the thirteenth and fourteenth centuries. The interests of the great landowners were not much at variance on either side of the frontier; in the nineteenth century they were agreed that Poland must never be allowed to regain her freedom. Bismarck, for example, shared all the Prussian nobleman's contempt for the Poles and sympathy for the Russians, even learning their language during his years in Petersburg.

An amusing description of Peter the Great's visit to the court of Prussia in the early eighteenth century is given by Frederick the Great's sister: 'The Czar, who was extremely fond of travelling, was on his way from Holland. Since he cared little for formalities or the rules of etiquette, he had asked the King for the use of a small country house belonging to the Queen. The Queen was not at all taken by this scheme and anticipating the chaos Russian visits tend to leave in their wake, she had the furniture and everything breakable removed. . . . The King and Queen received their guests by the riverside. As the Czar landed he stretched out his hand to the King saying: "I am delighted to see you, brother Frederick." He then approached the Queen and made as if to embrace her, which attempt she successfully foiled. . . . The Czarina introduced the Duke and Duchess of Mecklenburg who were accompanying her, and also the four hundred "ladies" of her court. These "ladies" were mostly German peasant-girls who served as chamber-maids, cooks, etc. Each of them bore a

c

richly clad child in her arms and on being asked if it were her own replied, indulging in a long sequence of Russian bows and curtseys, that "His Majesty had done her the honour." . . .' Frederick's sister continues: 'This barbarian pageant moved on two days later. The Queen hurried back to Monbijou. There she encountered the Destruction of Jerusalem—I have never seen anything like it. Everything was ruined; the Queen had to have the entire palace renovated.' Russians can be dangerous guests; it was left for a later generation in Berlin to find out just how dangerous.

But we must return to the Great Elector and seventeenth-century Berlin. He did much for Berlin, his capital: he repaired the Schloss and made good the damage done to the town during the Thirty Years War. Later, Queen Dorothea founded the suburb named after her, the Dorotheenstadt, and that named after her son, the Friedrichstadt, the first of those attempts at architectural planning that foreigners compared unkindly to a regiment of Prussian guards drawn up on parade. These two new sections were joined by an avenue of lime-trees, later to be the Unter den Linden. The Elector's policy of inviting skilled craftsmen to settle in Prussia quickly enriched the town and improved its outward appearance. Many new industries were introduced from Holland, thanks to the Elector's connection with the house of Orange. The rulers of Prussia were aware of the importance of a sound economy to the state they were trying to build, and the encouragement of trade was second only to the expansion of the army.

And the army expanded now at an alarming rate. From a mere 2,000 in 1640 it had grown to 8,000 at the end of the Thirty Years War, from 30,000 at the death of the Great Elector to 83,000 at the accession of Frederick the Great in 1740. By this date Prussia had, despite its minute size, acquired the fourth largest army in Europe and possibly the most efficiently led and organized. And as the Great Elector had foreseen, every increase in military power had been accompanied by an increase in political prestige. Brandenburg had become an eagerly sought ally. In 1700 her rulers were allowed to appropriate the title of King of Prussia with the tacit, if hardly enthusiastic, agreement of the Habsburg Emperor.

The new state soon became a patron of the arts and sciences in imitation of the court of Louis XIV. Queen Sophie Charlotte, consort of the first King of Prussia and one of the most cultured and accomplished women of her time, had built the Charlottenburg in what was still open country to the northwest of the town. There she entertained a man who was to be the first of a distinguished line of Berlin philosophers, a line that includes Fichte, Hegel and Marx. It was on Leibniz's recommendation that the Berlin Academy was set up and the foundation laid for that incongruous marriage of military might and intellectual prowess which was characteristic of nineteenth-century Berlin. An eighteenth-century Berliner, with the cheek of his race, spotted this incongruity while the Academy was being built—it was directly above the royal military stables —and remarked that the inscription should read '*Musis et Mulis*: a Latin joke, perhaps, but also the first recorded 'Berlinism'.

The first King of Prussia was fortunate to find in Andreas Schlüter a sculptor and architect to express the new-found glory of the Prussian state. Schlüter's statue of the Great Elector and his decorations to the Schloss brought the baroque style to Berlin and adapted it in the process—much as Wren had modified the southern style to his northern environment. The Royal Armoury is still standing on Unter den Linden, in its courtyard are Schlüter's famous 'Heads of Dying Warriors', perhaps his greatest achievement. These twisted agonized heads are a very frank statement of the real foundations of Prussia's glory, of the human price that has to be paid for political greatness. Their realism and harshness put them beside the work of Heinrich von Kleist as an expression of the Prussian spirit.

But Prussia, though already a power of some consequence, was not yet a great power, and Frederick the Great in his *History of the House of Brandenburg* chided his grandfather, the first King of Prussia, for providing his country with the externals of kingship before the foundations of real power had been laid. He praised on the other hand his own father, the Soldier King, a pious puritanical martinet who earned the hearty detestation of his subjects for his rigid subjection of all else to the welfare of his army. Yet what in other men could be reckoned a vice was in the case of the Soldier King a virtue. His miserliness was such that he could not bring himself to waste his precious six-foot grenadiers in any of the petty wars of his time. He contrived to be a Militarist without becoming an Aggressor. Frederick had no such scruples. And with his father's military power at his disposal, he could achieve what he believed was his mission: to make Prussia a Great Power. Frederick had been scarcely six months on the throne, when, in October 1740, he gave his troops the order to enter Silesia.

Chapter 3

FRIDERICUS REX

1740–1786

FREDERICK II of Prussia is the latest monarch considered by school history books to deserve the epithet 'the Great'. After him, as before him, there were Good kings and Bad kings, Strong kings and Weak kings, Bad kings who were Good men and vice versa; but there were to be no more Great kings. Peter of Russia had been a great king, and before him *le Roi Soleil*, Charles V of Austria, Elizabeth of England. The popular verdict was not generous with the title.

For greatness was not a quality generally expected of kings. In the tradition of Christendom a king was not to be judged by his works; he was a ruler by grace of God. Nor was it expected in practice; a Weak king (weak in the eyes of *1066 and All That*) could appoint ministers and marshals for the good of his realm and be no less a king. 'Greatness' was a work of supererogation. Indeed, when one considers history since the French Revolution one could wish that it had remained so, that the success principle had not come to be applied to heads of states. For while Napoleon and Hitler certainly have features in common with Frederick, they differ in an important way; they were usurpers and he a king by grace of God. Also, and this may be offered by way of apology for an extensive treatment of Frederick and his doings, the subjects of an absolute monarch seem to have no independent existence. He is not dependent on them for his position and they assume the form he imposes. The inhabitants of eighteenth-century London have a way of life apart from, even in opposition to the Court. But in Berlin, Vienna, or Petersburg the manners and morals of the capital reflect those prevailing in the King's entourage.

Under the Puritan regime of the Soldier King the Berliners are said to have been assiduous churchgoers; under Frederick free-thinking principles were expressed openly in the drawing-rooms. Nevertheless, the French taste dominant at Court first met with native resistance when Lessing worked in Berlin during the Seven Years War. And something of the Berliners' disrespectful wit lay always under the surface; indeed, Frederick had more than a touch of it himself. Frederick is, whichever way one looks at it, the most important figure in Prussia and in Berlin during his own long and adventurous reign. If Frederick was a Great king and a Great man it would be as well to examine his credentials.

It is worth insisting that the English prejudice against Frederick is of quite recent growth; it dates from August 1914. The storm of moral indignation then released against Frederick and 'Prussianism' in general is hard to account for; it is as though Englishmen had hidden their disapproval of Frederick's actions for a century and a half for reasons of diplomatic tact. During most of that period Prussia had been England's most reliable ally on the Continent.

Contemporary English reactions to Frederick's invasion and annexation of Silesia in 1740 varied from indifference—Silesia was one of 'those distant and small countries of which we do not know very much'—to reluctant admiration when Frederick defended himself against the rest of Europe in the Seven Years War. The numerous inns bearing the sign of the King of Prussia give the lie to our latter-day moralism. John Bull admired Fritz heartily. Bonfires were lit on the King's birthday in London. And, indeed, why not? While Fritz popped Silesia in his poacher's bag, John Bull was rounding up an Empire in Asia and the Americas. The going was still good, and Imperialism and Aggression were not yet everyday terms of abuse. It was useful to have someone to keep the French busy on the Continent, to wage war in one's own interest, if not on one's behalf, even if it did cost a good deal in subsidies.

Nevertheless, if ever there was a clear case of unprovoked aggression, it was Frederick's youthful decision to fling his father's superbly trained army into Silesia. He knew that Maria Theresa's succession was causing political difficulties in Vienna. It was the ideal moment for an attack on Austria. And Frederick made no secret of it; his aggression was launched simply and solely to force the recognition of Prussia as a great power in the European Concert. Frederick, in other words, was urged on by the desire for Greatness.

For it would be wrong to distinguish Frederick the man from Frederick the King of Prussia; state power was incarnate in him, and no man had more right to say 'l'état c'est moi'. His famous maxim that 'the King of Prussia is the first servant of his state' should not be interpreted in too abstract a way; the identification of King and State remained a very real thing. In a dispatch Frederick once gave instructions that in the event of capture 'the business of the state shall be carried on without regard to my personal safety', and added 'car je suis le roi lorsque je suis libre'. Frederick would have subscribed to the proposition 'freedom is responsibility'. Freedom meant for him ceaseless responsibility and decision, at every moment of his life and for every one of his subjects. Frederick was a tyrant, no doubt of it, but he was also the nearest approach among modern rulers to Plato's philosopher king.

Yet, essentially, he was not so much the originator of a new kind of kingship as the most thorough-going exponent of the old. He was an absolute monarch in the post-Lutheran tradition of Germany and in the Latin tradition of Machiavelli and

Louis XIV. The feudal element in Prussia was still very much alive, but the Great Elector had broken the power of the *Junkers* and ensured the loyalty to his person of the officer corps and nobility. Frederick represents, in fact, the culmination of absolute monarchy. He was guided by '*Raison d'état*' alone, the Enlightenment having eliminated the last vestiges of a 'Christian order of things'. His father would have hesitated to offend the Habsburgs whom he recognized as Emperors of Germany, his feudal overlords. Frederick was a *Realpolitiker* of the New Age. He saw that Prussia would have the best chances if she kept herself free from permanent commitments. She must exploit the divisions and shifts of power regardless of religious sympathy or racial solidarity. These principles had been clearly formulated in the Great Elector's Political Testament, and they ruled the practice of Frederick as they did that of Bismarck a century later. Yet in none of this was Frederick more than the most rational and competent exponent of a political ethic which had been dominant in Europe for centuries. In what, then, did his originality consist?

He was hailed, and is often remembered, as the first of the short-lived species of Enlightened Despots. That he was a Despot there is no reason to dispute. He was born to despotism, it was the universal and familiar system of government; and it is hardly a reflection on his character. His 'Enlightenment' should not be confused with Democracy or Liberalism. It meant in practice chiefly Religious Indifference: 'in my country everyone may work out his salvation as he pleases'. And this was a Toleration that in no way conflicted with *Raison d'état*. It led to a number of minor reforms, inspired by the much-invoked spirit of Humanity (in whose honour Frederick composed those interminable French verses it was Voltaire's duty to correct and improve). His first act as King, for instance, was to abolish judicial torture and to allow freedom of the press. But Voltaire, who held pacifist views, was somewhat at a loss to find that his professed admirer, whom he visited in the summer of 1740, had just invaded Silesia and initiated a European conflagration.

While Frederick cared nothing for what his subjects thought or wrote on theological matters, political necessity soon made him revise his first generous impulses. And, indeed, his Enlightenment was in part an expression of his contempt for human nature. Another saying of Frederick's runs: 'They can *say* what they like, so long as they let me *do* what I like.' It is a saying which shows how well he knew his Berliners, who have always been famous for their gift of the gab. Riding through the streets of the town one day he saw a crowd laughing and cheering at a placard hanging from a roof-top. On hearing that it depicted His Majesty with a large coffee-grinder between his knees (coffee was then highly taxed, much to the fury of the Berliners; there were even official coffee-sniffers who denounced coffee-drinkers to the police), Frederick rode up and ordered the placard to be hung lower 'so that the people should see it properly'. The crowd was monstrously delighted and gave three rousing cheers for His Majesty as he rode away.

Like many great rulers Frederick was a great actor and had an accomplished actor's contempt-through-familiarity for his audience. But with Frederick it went deeper. He sadly remarked to his protégé, de Catt, during the Seven Years War that 'he feared man was made for action rather than for thought'—a hidden depth of pessimism in the former eulogist of Humanity! But to Frederick, Enlightenment did not mean exactly what it meant to those enthusiasts who danced round the Tree of Liberty a quarter of a century later. It was perhaps at bottom a determination to be deceived by nothing, a radical Nietzschean scepticism, a wish to strip reality bare. Riding into the city as an old man, in a shabby blue uniform and cocked hat, after acknowledging the cheers of the populace he snapped to his adjutant: 'They would cheer just the same for an old monkey in uniform.'

Yet, like many great men, Frederick was a convert. He was

not so much a Prussian by birth as by conviction and faith. And perhaps it is here, and not in his confessed Enlightenment or his conquests, that his originality and the profound fascination of his character lie. The story of his childhood has often been told; the savage maltreatment by a father who was determined to force him into his own mould, philistine, puritan, military. Frederick like so many sensitive children found refuge in music and literature, particularly the poetry and drama of the *grand siècle* and of Voltaire. Even during the most desperate periods of the Seven Years War he found time to chuckle over a blasphemous epigram of Voltaire's or treat his generals to an evening's recital of Racine. For Frederick, like Napoleon and on an abysmally lower level, Hitler, had at bottom an artist's nature. Not that his verses were good; on the contrary, even Voltaire's elaborate flattery could not persuade him that they were. But he had the typical qualities of the artist as man-of-action; dangerous qualities, as he admitted himself when he said that 'if he wished to punish a province with great severity he would appoint a scribbler to govern it'.

The father could hardly be expected to foresee such a development. He saw merely that his son spent his time scribbling verses and contemplating, no doubt profanely, the delights of philosophy. He had even cajoled his tutor, contrary to the strictest royal instructions, into giving him Latin lessons. The Prussian King considered political economy more useful to a prince than any dead language, but again he could not foresee the effect of Plutarch and Caesar on the romantic mind of his son. Frederick had much that was German in his character. The exclusive admiration for a foreign culture was not the least German feature of his mind. And his wit was not the Frenchman's natural levity—there was more than enough of this among his disreputable table companions at Sanssouci—his wit had something distinctly metaphysical, not to say Mephistophelian about it. In early life Frederick must have shared that mental state portrayed over and over again in

Goethe's *Wilhelm Meister* and the other German *Bildungs-romane*: that profound, frustrating and ultimately creative confusion of the youthful mind.

Literary parallels suggest themselves at once: Frederick as Hamlet or Frederick as the companion of Falstaff. And there is in German literature a still closer parallel, Heinrich von Kleist's *Prince of Homburg*. This play contains the *locus classicus* of a 'conversion' to what may loosely be called Prussianism. Von Kleist, who wrote the play in Berlin shortly before his suicide in 1810, describes how his youthful hero, nephew of the Great Elector, sleep-walking in the palace gardens on the night before a battle against the Swedes, weaves himself a crown of laurels in anticipation of glory. On the battlefield the Prince, still bemused by his dream of the night before, ignores the express command of the Elector and launches an attack. The attack is successful and the Prussians drive the Swedes from the field. But the Prince has disobeyed orders and is placed under arrest. A court martial demands the usual penalty for insubordination in the Prussian army: the death sentence.

In a scene reminiscent of the prison scene in *Measure for Measure* the Prince, confronted with his empty tomb, breaks down; any fate, even the most dishonourable, is to be preferred to the horror of death. His betrothed Natalie pleads for his life, but the Great Elector argues that to pardon the Prince would be to put the Prussian state at the mercy of anarchy, that anarchy which in the Thirty Years War men had come to fear more than death. This dialogue reads like a Prussian catechism, though touched with Kleist's sophisticated irony. Natalie cries:

> First crown him as a victor, then behead him—
> Does History demand this feat from you?
> Oh, that were so sublime, my dearest uncle,
> That some might call it Inhumanity,
> And God created none so merciful as thee . . .

Then, as the Elector hears of the Prince's collapse at the prospect of death, he offers him his freedom on one condition:

if the Prince still considers the verdict passed upon him to have
been unjust. But the Prince now refuses to accept pardon on
these terms. He too recognizes the necessity of the rule of law.
He too affirms the Prussian state:

> I will exalt the Articles of War
> Which I transgressed before the army then
> And sanction them through freely chosen death . . .
> What could that victory be which I
> Might yet wrest from the Swede, compared to that . . .
>   . . . over the vilest
> Enemies within, defiance and presumption,
> That I shall win tomorrow?

The Prince calmly awaits execution, he has reconciled himself to those ideals of duty, honour, obedience that he pro-
claims as the very condition of the ordered life. A dramatic
change of heart has been effected, the romantic dreamer has
been converted into a Prussian.

Now there is a remarkably similar incident in Frederick's
own life. Finding life at Court unbearable as a young man (he
had to submit to the strictest discipline, yet was allowed to
share in the business of government) he had conspired with two
young lieutenants, the English Ambassador conniving, to run
away to England. When the plan became known, one managed
to escape, but Frederick and his other accomplice were placed
under close arrest. The King wished the culprits to be charged
with desertion from the army; and in an army which lost more
soldiers by desertion than on the field of battle the death penalty was certain for this offence. For a time the Court feared for
the Prince's life. But after much searching of conscience—for
the Soldier King was a pious Calvinist and was no doubt also
anxious about the succession—the King decided on an alter-
native means of punishment that bears an uncanny resemblance
to Kleist's play. He ordered the execution of Frederick's
friend to be carried out under his prison window in the
fortress of Küstrin and instructed that the young prince be

held at the window, for his edification, by two stout Prussian grenadiers.

That this terrible experience was the turning-point in Frederick's life is likely enough. Many of his remarks to de Catt in later years reveal the existence of this trauma. Thus, on the 7th of July 1759: 'The King was in low spirits, spoke frequently of his father and it was clear enough how former sufferings had branded his sensitive and lively spirit. "How few joys have I known," said the King, "and what an ocean of care. And even when I experience something of a pleasant nature, the image of my father comes into my mind to disturb the enjoyment. How cruelly he treated me! Yet despite all my sufferings I have always admired him and valued his excellent qualities. . . ."' The modern reader can scarcely refrain at this point from the urge to psychoanalyse. But neither the Prussian ethic nor any other can be disposed of so easily.

And Frederick's experience was certainly not unique. Prussianism was the secular religion that filled the vacuum left by the decay of Protestantism in Northern Germany. G. K. Chesterton called Prussia 'a patch of eighteenth-century heresy'. (It is perhaps the only religion still actively expanding, if it is legitimate to draw up the genealogy Frederick—Hegel—Marx—Lenin.) The religion of the State was not new, but Frederick was an illustrious convert to its anti-humanist assumptions; his political success was a chief agent in propagating it over Germany. It has left—that is why we discuss it—an indelible imprint on the development of Berlin.

But the Iron Prussian was only one side of Frederick's character. As Voltaire remarked on arriving at Sanssouci: 'It was Sparta in the morning and Athens in the afternoon.' The King kept Spartan hours. He rose in summer at three, attended to correspondence and practised on the flute. He made it his business to examine in detail the work of every department of state; he was especially interested in all building projects and in the maintenance of the splendid army he had inherited. In foreign affairs, too, all the decisions were his own; his ministers had merely to carry out the schemes of his brilliant but utterly lonely and inaccessible mind. The human weaknesses which from time to time caused friction even in the well-oiled clockwork of the Prussian state seldom escaped the eye of that cynical connoisseur of human nature.

Perhaps, like other despisers of the human race, he hoped to find Man's lost innocence again in Art. Frederick's patronage and love of the arts is often thought to be an incongruity in his character—as though despots from Nero to Adolf Hitler had not all shown this *faible* for the arts. More surprising—for every German princeling of the age was building his miniature Versailles, his Sanssouci or Solitude—more surprising is the passion with which he sought to keep Voltaire at his court long after personal intercourse with him had sapped admiration for his character, if not for his work. Their relationship had begun with a fanfare of compliments. Voltaire had written at Frederick's accession to the throne:

> Enfin voici le jour le plus beau de ma vie
> Que le monde attendait et que vous seul craignez,
> Le grand jour ou la terre est par vous embellit,
>   Le jour ou vous reignez.
>
> Quelle est du Dieu vivant la veritable image?
> Vous, des talents, des arts et des vertus l'appui,
> Vous, Salomon du Nord, plus savant et plus sage
>   Et moins faible que lui.

To which Frederick had replied gracefully:

> Desormais ce people que j'aime
> Est l'unique Dieu que je sais,
> Adieu mes vers et mes concerts
> Tous les plaisirs, Voltaire même;
> Mon devoir est mon Dieu suprême.

It was not, of course, the whole picture. *Devoir* might have become Frederick's *Dieu suprême*, but the pleasures of life were not given up, they were rather postponed until dinner-time. And the greatest of these pleasures—for Frederick was a life-long misogynist—remained the evening battle of wits with Voltaire. Round the dinner-table at Sanssouci sat a number of other *bel esprits*. De la Mettrie, the atheist doctor, who had been expelled from France for his book *L'Homme machine*, and who would pursue Frederick with his practical jokes into places 'where even kings are generally permitted some privacy'. More respectable, though with a less ready wit, was the scientist Maupertuis, whom Frederick had made president of the Academy and who was to be the occasion of the final break between Voltaire and his royal master.

For, at bottom, however brilliant as intellectual sparring partners, Frederick and Voltaire were heartless old cynics between whom little love was lost. On his first visit, Voltaire was naïve enough to suppose he could extract some state secrets over the dinner-table for transmission to the court of France. It was, of course, a vain hope. Frederick was tight as an oyster in such matters and was perfectly well aware of Voltaire's little scheme, which afforded him much amusement. And Voltaire's servility was deceptive; he hated being the paid retainer of any king, however enlightened. He was also jealous of Maupertuis' reputation and wrote a spiteful attack on one of the unfortunate man's more fanciful hypotheses. Frederick was furious. On a previous visit Voltaire had become involved in a shady financial transaction with a Berlin Jew, a matter which had come into the courts. Now he had held up to ridicule the head of the Prussian Academy. Frederick thereupon dropped the remark to de la Mettrie, relying on its immediate transmission to Voltaire: 'When you have sucked an orange, you throw away the peel.' Voltaire chose the King's most sensitive sport for his counter-thrust: 'Does the man expect me to go on washing his dirty linen for ever?' This in reference to some verses he had received for correction.

Voltaire was by this time, 1753, ready to leave Prussia; and we may wonder why Frederick made such frantic efforts to retain the presence of a man he habitually described as a monkey and a scoundrel. It seems that he genuinely wished to be able to write good French verse and was convinced that only Voltaire could show him how. But there were limits to the patience of the *Salomon du Nord*. When Voltaire reprinted the attack on Maupertuis in Leipzig against his express orders, Frederick had it burned by the public hangman. The culprit himself made off in a south-westerly direction with a copy of the King's verses which he would certainly have given to the world had they not been recovered by the combined efforts of the Prussian excise and secret police. It was an appropriate ending to their relationship, intellectually so brilliant and personally so squalid.

Yet Voltaire's years in Berlin (strictly speaking in Potsdam, for Frederick preferred to the capital itself the small garrison town his father had built to the south-west of the city) were not without influence on the city. It is true that he had little personal contact with its inhabitants, nor after his first escapade can the King have wished him to. Ignorance of German on the other hand would in itself have been no hindrance; French was the normal language of the educated, not to speak of the numerous Huguenot refugees. Yet if Prussia possessed in Frederick the most civilized king in Europe it possessed in the Prussian *Junkers* the most barbarian nobility. The *Junkers*, even more than their counterparts in England, were country-bred and bound to the feudal way of life in Pomerania and East Prussia and the March of Brandenburg. Very few could afford to build themselves town houses in Berlin, though some were forced to do so by Frederick for reasons of prestige. Patronage of the arts was therefore hardly to be expected of them—rather of the rich cultured Jewish families who benefited from Frederick's Enlightenment. The land itself was too poor and there were no great landowners wealthy enough to match the Esterhazys in Hungary, the patrons of Haydn.

Court patronage, too, though it could be generous, was dictated solely by the personal taste of the monarch. Frederick gave great sums for the purchase of works of art, classical statues, French and Italian paintings; and he employed many excellent architects and craftsmen for his ambitious projects. The face of Berlin changed greatly during his reign. Knobels-dorff built the opera house on Unter den Linden and Frederick's Italian Opera was soon considered one of the best in Europe. Frederick's brother, Prince Henry, built his palace on the other side of the road (this fine eighteenth-century building is now the Humboldt, *i.e.* the Eastern University: the Opera House has also been rebuilt after destruction in the war). Berlin was gradually becoming a handsome, if somewhat too geo-metrical city, Potsdam a 'Georgian' town as beautiful in its way as Bath.

But though the King's taste was good—he built Sanssouci himself and put finishing touches to many designs in his auto-cratic way—his taste was limited, and limited in a way that was unfortunate for the people he governed. For in art, too, Frederick was not really the first of the new but the last of the old. Sanssouci is in the style of the contemporary French Rococo, and with Antoine Pesne's murals and the Chinese tea-house the result is charming enough. But it was no more original than the King's French verses. In music, it is true, his taste was more catholic. There was a famous meeting with Johann Sebastian Bach, the occasion of the *Musical Offering*. Bach was, incidentally, one of the few eminent Germans of the time to see the inside of Sanssouci. He had written his Branden-burg Concertos for a music-loving Hohenzollern some twenty years before; his son Carl Philipp Emanuel became *Kapell-meister* to Frederick, who thus made Berlin a pioneer of the new music of Haydn and Mozart.

The *Singspiel*, which was later to reach its apotheosis in Vienna with Mozart's *Magic Flute*, started its triumphal course in 1743 with *Der Teufel ist los* in Berlin. This was itself a

D

translation of a ballad-farce *The Devil to Pay* performed at
Drury Lane in 1731; a follow-on of the *Beggar's Opera* that so
delighted the Prussian ambassador that he adapted it for the
Berlin stage. Curiously enough the music for Gay's *Beggar's
Opera* was arranged by Johann Pepusch, a Berliner, and clearly
many Berliners and Londoners preferred this type of enter-
tainment to the splendours of Italian opera. If the musical
life of Berlin in the mid-eighteenth century was active and
fruitful, this was to some extent Frederick's doing. But in
literature his taste was narrow. He wholly failed to appreciate
the beginning of a new age of German literature in the works
of Lessing, Klopstock and Goethe. A fact all the stranger in that
he himself had done so much to restore German national pride
and self-confidence.

 If a Great king is expected to bequeath some aesthetic monument of his Greatness, Frederick must be admitted to have
failed. In a later chapter we shall consider whether a 'Prussian
style' exists, whether the classical strength and simplicity of the
Brandenburger Tor (built in 1791) or Schinkel's somewhat
later Neue Wache corresponds in some way to the 'Prussian
virtues'. Certainly French Rococo does not. It is one of the
comic incongruities of Sanssouci to find the uncouth war-
horse, General von Ziethen, dominating the silk hangings and
gold tracery of the royal cabinet. Von Ziethen was a true son
of the March, rustic, hard and monosyllabic, with a great
reputation for courage and resourcefulness in his doings with
the enemy. He could never have felt at home in the pretty-
pretty architecture of Sanssouci. And apart from the war-songs
of Gleim and of Ewald von Kleist, another member of the great
Kleist clan, there is no literary or architectural monument to
the epic struggle of the Seven Years War in which Ziethen took
part. And for this Frederick himself was partly responsible.

 The King's views on German art were simple: there was
none worth mentioning. '*Götz von Berlichingen*, imitation
détestable de ces mauvaises pièces Anglaises', he wrote of

Goethe's first play on its first performance in Berlin; thereby condemning not only that 'Northern savage' Shakespeare but the coming literature of his own nation. Goethe confesses in his autobiography to a boyish enthusiasm for Frederick's exploits: all Frankfurt knew him to be '*fritzisch*'. And he remarks of Frederick's victories: 'The Prussians and with them the whole of Protestant Germany had won a great treasure for our literature. . . . The first real contact with life entered German poetry with Frederick the Great and his deeds in the Seven Years War. Every national literature becomes stale that does not spring from contact with human events. Kings should be portrayed in times of war and danger. . . . It is then that they monopolize our interests, for then they not only determine human destiny, but also share it, thus becoming more interesting to us than the Gods themselves who indeed determine human destiny but are not involved in the consequences. Every nation, if she desires to be esteemed in the world, must have her epic period. . . .'

And of Berlin, Goethe goes on to remark: 'Already thanks to the French colony and the King's preference for the culture of this nation and their system of taxation' (a hit at the notorious tax-farming which Frederick had introduced) 'a quantity of French culture had come to Prussia, which was no bad thing for the Germans in that it challenged them to emulate and resist it. Frederick's dislike of things German was a piece of luck for the development of our literature.' A piece of luck, in that the new literature was compelled to measure itself against the established culture of France; but also perhaps because the tender shoots of German culture might have withered in the shadow of so autocratic a patron.

And in fact the German genius had found another patron and another mentor: in the Berlin *bourgeoisie* and in the person of Gotthold Ephraim Lessing. Lessing, a generation older than Goethe and a Saxon by birth, was living in Berlin during the 'fifties and 'sixties; and it was in Berlin that he planned and carried out a literary counterpart to Frederick's raid on Silesia. His aim was, like Frederick's, to redistribute the balance of power, to increase the wealth of his state by annexation of a rich neighbouring province, in this case, Shakespeare and the English drama. Shakespeare was not, of course, unknown in Germany; but it was Lessing who first saw that Shakespeare was the missing father of German literature, the dramatist who could redeem the years of Babylonish captivity. Lessing felt that of all the world's poets Shakespeare was the most 'Germanic', just as the poets and architects of eighteenth-century France were the least. And Lessing saw that the former could be employed to drive out the latter. Here the rising middle classes could be depended upon for support. The taste of the Berlin *bourgeoisie* was not Frederick's. At the performance of *Götz von Berlichingen* Frederick noted with horror: 'La parterre applaudit et demande avec enthusiasme la répétition de ce dégoûtant platitude.'

With his friends Friedrich Nicolai, bookseller and renowned *lumière* of Berlin, and Moses Mendelssohn, the Jewish philosopher, he began to publish his *Letters Concerning the most recent Literature*. In these he criticized the French theatre of the day and championed the cause of the English. But Lessing was soon to do more. He began to write plays himself. Two of these, *Miss Sarah Sampson*—the title betrays the English influence—and the charming *Minna von Barnhelm*, were produced by Doebbelin, the new theatrical director. By putting these first-fruits of the German drama on the stage, Doebbelin became the ancestor of a long and distinguished line of actor-managers in Berlin, from Iffland to Brahm and Max Reinhardt.

If Kleist's *Prince of Homburg* is Prussia's great tragedy, *Minna von Barnhelm* is her great comedy. Von Tellheim, Lessing's hero, is an officer discharged in allegedly dishonourable circumstances after the Seven Years War. Having lost both his source of income and—what is worse, for he is a Prussian officer—his honour, von Tellheim determines never to see his

betrothed again. But the resourceful Minna at once hurries to
Berlin. By giving von Tellheim to believe that she is being
persecuted by a wicked uncle she makes him forget his un-
worthiness in defence of her cause. The piece is witty and
economical, and though poking gentle fun at its hero's exaggerated sense of honour, presents von Tellheim as a most convincing and attractive Prussian. Lessing had won the first
decisive battle in his Silesian campaign; it was for his successors
to exploit the rich resources of the newly won territory.

But the Berlin middle classes, though already to some extent
patrons of the arts, and of the German arts, were still excluded
from any political or military share in the fortunes of Prussia.
Lessing writes to a friend: 'How can one feel well in Berlin?
Everything one sees there makes one's gorge rise. Don't talk
to me about your "Berlin freedoms" to think and to write.
It boils down quite simply to the freedom to make as many
tasteless remarks about religion as one likes. But let someone
get up in Berlin to defend the rights of the subject and attack
exploitation and despotism, as happens daily in France or in
Denmark, and you'll soon see which country in Europe is
today the most abjectly enslaved.'

In a similar vein Goethe, visiting Berlin during a war crisis
in 1778, had written back to Frau von Stein in Weimar: 'It's a
curious feeling to be present at the springs of War just at the
moment when they threaten to overflow . . . the splendour of
the royal city, its life and order and abundance, which would
be nothing without the tens of thousands of human beings
ready to be sacrificed. Men, horses, wagons, guns, ammunition:
the streets are full of them. If only I could describe adequately
the monstrous piece of clock-work spread out here before one's
eyes! From the movements of the puppets one infers the
existence of hidden wheels and in particular the ancient,
mighty wheel with F.R. on it that is responsible for the movement of all the others.'

Such was Frederick's Berlin, seen through the eyes of one

who had lived there and those of an occasional visitor. Goethe once referred to the people of Berlin as 'ein verwegener Menschenschlag'—'a dare-devil race'; and we begin to be aware of the presence of a fourth estate in these years. The vast growth of population—from 90,000 at Frederick's accession to 150,000 at his death—began to shape Berlin into the proletarian city we meet a century and a half later. But the most surprising thing is that Berlin preserved her identity at all considering the diversity of her elements: German peasants from the March, Czech and Austrian Protestant refugees, Dutch craftsmen, French Huguenots, Jews from East and West, a handful of Jacobites, and later the flood of Polish Catholic immigrants.

Yet the Bear and the Eagle, the two fixed poles in Berlin's history, were already present: the Berliner himself with his cockney humour and voluble disrespect; and the Prussian Eagle, now fierce and warlike, now benevolent and protective. And there must have been fusion of a sort, too, for the Seven Years War saw the birth of a Prussian nation. The Berliners are not immune, then as now, from bouts of hero-worship; and it was to Frederick alone that the new nation owed its position as a great power in Europe. However we may judge Frederick, it is hard not to agree with Goethe, when he says that such rulers must compel our interest in that 'they determine the lives of their subjects down to the last detail'—a true judgement of Frederick, the indefatigable worker and jealous taskmaster of all departments of state. But they also compel our interest because, in Goethe's words, 'they not only determine human destiny, but also share it, thus becoming more interesting to us than the Gods themselves who indeed determine human destiny but are not involved in the consequences'. Could a better apology for history's preoccupation with Frederick and its granting of the title Great be found than in this remark of Goethe's?

Chapter 4

THE EAGLE AS PHOENIX
1786–1815

'17TH AUGUST 1786. A mood of silence, though not of mourning; the people seem numbed rather than sorrowful. One sees scarcely a face that does not wear an expression of relief, even of hope. No voice of regret is to be heard; not a sigh, not a word of praise! Is this the sum of so many victorious battles, of such fame and glory? Is this the end of almost half a century of rule, a reign so rich in great deeds?'

Such were Mirabeau's impressions of the funeral of the Great King, to whose court he had been sent to carry out a 'secret mission'. The mission was not, in fact, carried out with any great secrecy; Mirabeau took the opportunity of meeting the great men of Prussia in society, where he was received with the respect due to a French *bel esprit*. The letters he wrote back to Talleyrand are a curious mixture of low scandal and high political speculation. Yet there is a political purpose in the way he assiduously picks up and relays the stray gossip of the court: 'The new King makes it his habit to retire at half-past nine in the evening—the Pietist faction at Court is much in evidence—evidently the King has thrown off the excesses of his youth.' But truth will out. It appears that at half-past nine the King is accustomed to retire, not to the Royal Bedchamber, but to a remote wing of the Palace where he can carry on his debauches.

Mirabeau notes that the new King—Frederick William II—cuts a poor figure on horseback at military parades, does not attend to correspondence regularly, is afraid of being dominated by favourites, and like many rulers of despotic states has a decided preference for tame second-rate men as his ministers. Mirabeau, the last foreigner to be received in audience, had been a profound admirer of the dead king and recognized these symptoms for what they were: the beginning of the decline of the delicately balanced structure of Frederick's Prussia.

Prussia was still what Frederick had made it, the cornerstone of the European state system. Yet could it maintain this position without a king who was at the same time a soldier and statesman of genius? Mirabeau thought not. He was altogether sceptical about the political foundations of Prussian power. He coined the *bon mot*: 'Prussia is not a state that possesses an army, but an army that possesses a state.' Yet Berlin was now, as it had been in the Seven Years War and as it was to be again in 1813, in 1870, and in 1945, the power-pivot of Europe, half-way between Paris and Moscow.

And Mirabeau was caused to reflect on the future significance of Russian power by tales he heard in Berlin of Russian expeditions to Astrakhan and perhaps to India. 'How many revolutions, how much human and material strife will be occasioned by the expansion of this Empire that successively overawes and enslaves all surrounding nations? What species of understanding must the Emperor of Austria possess if he cannot see that the Turks and the Poles are less dangerous neighbours to him than this strange people with such infinite potentialities, who are open to every influence, who become the best soldiers in the world and are of all human beings the most malleable?' Mirabeau's reflections seem prophetic indeed to the foreign observer in the Berlin of the 1950's.

'The power-pivot of Europe'—and the perennial listening-

post for official and unofficial 'spies' of other nations. Mirabeau's reports may or may not have had a permanent influence
on the foreign policy of France; but the decline of Prussia
ending in the disastrous defeat at Jena and dismemberment after
the Treaty of Tilsit followed the pattern he had foreseen.
Mirabeau saw that Prussia was not a nation in the English or in
the French revolutionary sense. The Prussian peasantry, he
remarked, if their enfranchisement were proclaimed to them,
would undoubtedly reply: 'We are very much obliged to you
for our enfranchisement, but we do not choose to be free.'
Similarly, the Berlin *bourgeoisie* did not identify its fortunes
with those of the dynasty under which it lived. So that while a
Danton could rouse the French middle classes to patriotic
fervour, Prussia's defeat in the field must lead to her political
extinction. But Mirabeau's report was coldly received in Paris
at the time. Versailles needed the good will of the Court of
Berlin and the scandalous revelations of the Comte de Mirabeau
were disposed of by the public hangman when they appeared
in book form—which did not prevent the printing of numerous
pirated editions, particularly in Saxony, where the *Secret
Memoirs of the Court of Berlin* were read with undisguised
Schadenfreude.

Frederick the Great's successor has fared badly with the
historians of the house of Hohenzollern: he was lazy, bad-
tempered, licentious, superstitious; as unlike his uncle as a man
can well be. And, indeed, his life was oppressed by the comparison. It was as if he knew of Frederick's contempt for him
and was driven by a kind of defiance, born of weakness, to
deserve it. Yet the reaction from the older Prussian Spartanism
and Puritanism was in itself human enough, and the reign of
Frederick William II [1786–1797], like that of Charles II of
England, was a much-needed respite.

Of his great-nephew, Frederick William III [1797–1840], on
the other hand, Frederick had once said: 'I shall reign again
in him.' And his accession in 1797 seemed to give hope for the

future of Prussia. His young queen, the adored Queen Louise of Prussia, who occupies to this day a place in the hearts of all true Prussians equal to that of Mary Queen of Scots among admirers of the House of Stuart—Louise restored to Potsdam something of the glamour it had lost at the death of the great king. But her simplicity and charm, her patronage of the arts, her courage in adversity, which aroused the admiration of Napoleon himself, these things alone could not restore the prestige of the Prussian crown. Her husband, though honourable and dutiful in a humdrum Prussian way, combined as a ruler the qualities of stubbornness and irresolution. If the Hohenzollerns alternated between austerity and ostentation in private and public life, Frederick William III belonged once again to the Spartan contingent. A true son of the March, he carried thrift into his choice of language. The clipped speech of the officer corps and a somewhat limited vocabulary produced curious effects—as when he dismissed the royal orchestra with the barrack-square comment: 'Damned fine playing this evening, gentlemen!' And, indeed, none of the Hohenzollerns after Frederick the Great was of more than average ability. The preservation of Frederick's legacy lay in other men's hands: with statesmen like Baron vom Stein and Bismarck, soldiers like Gneisenau, Scharnhorst, Clausewitz and Moltke.

The years following the death of Frederick the Great are the most fascinating in German intellectual history. At Weimar Goethe and Schiller were tending the young plant of German Classicism. In nearby Jena the Schlegel brothers and Novalis were busily clearing the ground for that Romantic reversal of values which was to dominate European art for a century. It is not always easy to say where Romanticism begins and Classicism stops, nor whether it is subject matter or style which this terminology is supposed to define. It is particularly confusing in Germany, where Classicism and Romanticism were born together and developed side by side—even within the mind of a single artist. When Goethe remarked 'Classicism is health and Romanticism is sickness', he was looking back ironically on his own *Werther* and *Götz von Berlichingen*. Schinkel, whose Neue Wache on Unter den Linden is the acme of Prussian Classicism, moved in the Romantic salons in Berlin and painted extremely Pre-Raphaelite medieval townscapes. The worship of the Middle Ages and the worship of Ancient Greece were really two aspects of the same movement, a movement springing from a class which had so far played little part in German history. Through it the German *bourgeoisie* was to find its voice and begin to act on the national life. If Weimar and Jena were the cradles of the movement, it was from Berlin that the lusty infant could make its voice heard far beyond the frontiers of Germany.

In the autumn of 1792, two young Berliners, Ludwig Tieck, the son of an artisan, and Wilhelm Wackenroder, whose father had been burgomaster of the city, undertook an expedition on foot to the south of Germany. Young Tieck and Wackenroder enthused indiscriminately over the marvels of the past: the great churches of Franconia and Bavaria, the picturesque gabled houses of Bamberg and Nuremberg, towns that still breathed something of the long-departed glories of the medieval Emperors. Nuremberg particularly, then the best preserved medieval town in Europe, was an enchantment and a revelation. The mighty Albrecht Dürer became their ideal of what a German artist should be: humble, pious, craftsmanlike, incorruptible, recording the lives of the people in their daily work and in their commerce with the higher powers.

Certainly the contrast between the barrack-like architecture of their home town and this ancient Catholic civilization must have come as a shock to them. And it was this shock that initiated the Romantic movement. Tieck and Wackenroder saw in this older civilization something that could fill the spiritual vacuum of those North German states whose native religion—though not music—had long been in decay. This older culture was, significantly enough, not only authentically

German in origin, but also *bourgeois*. Its great lords and ladies seemed to the young Romantics immeasurably more attractive than the *Junkers* of their native Berlin. Under the impressions of this journey, Wackenroder composed his *Musings of an Art-loving Lay-brother*, that Burne-Jonesian first-fruit of the German Romantic movement. His devoted companion contrived to get this work published after Wackenroder's early death in 1798. It was the period when Wordsworth and Coleridge were living at Nether Stowey, hatching another literary revolution. Everywhere Rousseau and *Werther* were triumphant and Nicolai, the Berlin watch-dog of the Enlightenment, and the Rationalists were in full retreat.

If Wackenroder was the first martyr of the movement (the English reader is reminded of Chatterton), Tieck was its St. George. In his *Puss in Boots* Tieck let fly with Romantic high spirits and Romantic irony at the hard-headed burghers of Berlin. And, as with Brecht's *Threepenny Opera* in the 1920's, the burghers laughed innocently at a caricature of themselves intended by its author to be deadly. But the true stronghold of the movement was the university of Jena where Fichte lectured and Friedrich and August Wilhelm Schlegel organized and steeled its warriors for their battle with the *Zeitgeist*. Indeed, to the reader brought up on the English Romantics all too much time and energy seem to have been wasted on these war-like preparations, these interminable arguments as to the nature of art and the function of criticism. With the splendid exception of Novalis, it is surprising how little work of lasting value was created by the early German Romantics. In the first generation there was too much of Coleridge and too little of Wordsworth.

But the new faith had been proclaimed and the first converts won. August Wilhelm Schlegel was a born diplomat and business manager, no bad leader for a motley crew of hot-headed Transcendentalists and medieval dreamers. Lessing and his friends had campaigned for a national German drama freed from the tyranny of the French and borrowing from the English, above all from Shakespeare. And during these years at Jena, Tieck and August Wilhelm Schlegel were providing Germany with a translation of Shakespeare not unworthy of the original. Leaving brother Friedrich ruminating on the ultimate mysteries, the more active August Wilhelm set off to Berlin in 1801 to deliver the *Lectures on Literature and the Fine Arts* that were to influence Coleridge's criticism so profoundly. Just then Madame de Staël reached Berlin on one of her cultural foraging expeditions through Germany, Napoleon's armies close in her rear. It was in Berlin that she made a scoop that was also perhaps, in view of the later success of *De l'Allemagne* in France, German Romanticism's greatest triumph. She engaged August Wilhelm as tutor to her children and carried him off with her to the Lake of Geneva.

Napoleon was approaching. The ambiguous peace Prussia had enjoyed for a decade while France and Austria struggled was at last to be broken. The fruits of this peace had been twofold. Germany had experienced a truly Elizabethan decade that was to make up for the centuries during which her national literature had been stagnant. But the 'Holy Roman Empire of the German Nation' that had survived more than the gibes of Voltaire during the thousand years of its history, was on the point of dissolution. Not that the new writers mourned its passing. The new *bourgeois* culture had as yet little connection with the world of politics and the life of the nation as a whole. The successors of Frederick the Great, though more generous than he as patrons of German theatre and the German arts, never thought of looking to the rising middle classes for political support. Prussia's danger, clear to Mirabeau as early as 1786, was not apparent to her rulers.

The Prussian generals and the old noble families of the March—the von Kleists, the von Bredows, the von der Marwitz's, the von der Goltz's, the von Bülows—were still living in the after-glow of Frederick's victories. The bureaucratic state machine built up in the previous century was now hallowed by age and the memory of the military triumphs it had made possible. Yet even a state founded on the most impeccable rationalism, on the assumptions of *L'homme machine*, may succumb to the superstition of those who inherit it. The military principle had become 'what was good enough for Fritz is good enough for us': from the fixed battle order to recruitment of mercenaries and gauntlet-running. Much that Frederick had introduced was preserved although the national armies of the revolutionary era had long since rendered it out of date.

Prussia's own attitude to the revolution had been hopelessly indecisive. She had taken part with Austria at first in the wars of intervention and then retired to lick her wounds, leaving Austria to quell the forces of revolution alone. During the years leading up to 1806 she had watched Austria's piecemeal destruction from an easy and indeed shameful neutrality. But her own destruction was to follow in 1806. The Prussian army had marched out of Berlin fully confident of its superiority to the 'amateur' soldiers of the French revolution. Had not General von Möllendorf, its commander-in-chief, been one of Frederick's dashing young colonels? The handsome Prince Louis Ferdinand, glittering young hope of the House of Prussia and an enthusiast for the new German literature in Rahel Levin's salon in Berlin, had ridden gaily out of the city to join his regiment. So great was the confidence of the army and so great the actual defeat inflicted on it by Napoleon that rumours of a Prussian reverse in the neighbourhood of Jena, trickling back to the capital, were met with incomprehension and derision.

It is said that in these days Goethe, who took no more notice than his poetic contemporaries of political and military events, was absorbed at Weimar in the work of completing *Faust*. The downfall of Prussia was not an event to disturb the Olympian in putting the finishing touches to a drama he had worked on for thirty years. And Goethe's reaction was also that of the ostensibly 'true blue' burghers of Berlin. They were informed by Count von der Schulenburg, Governor of the city, that 'The King has lost a battle. The first duty of every citizen is to keep calm.' This celebrated order was taken all too literally. The King had lost a battle—that was his affair; the citizens' duty was to keep calm and wait upon events. As soon as it became plain that Napoleon would be allowed to occupy Berlin unopposed, the Prussian authorities made ready to evacuate the city. The garrison withdrew to the east across the river Oder, leaving the Berliners at the mercy of the conqueror.

One of them has described the entry of Napoleon: 'In the pomp of his suite of generals and marshals, you would scarcely have recognized the mighty one of the earth in his incon-spicuous grey cloak—had not the reverence shown by his entourage proved that it was he. In front of the Brandenburger Tor he glanced up for a moment at the Goddess of Victory, commemorating the four victories of Prussia over his own nation. . . . The earnestness of his face is seldom broken by a smile; and yet he has a strange smile, quite peculiar to him, a smile that does not permit others to smile when they stand in his presence. I saw him smile like that once during the entry into Berlin, when he heard not only his own troops shouting "Vive l'empereur" but also a large number of the Berliners themselves.'

It has often been remarked that between the decay of the medieval *Reich* and the Second *Reich* created by Bismarck, no people could have been less warlike and aggressive than the Germans (something similar has been said of the Japanese). So much for 'racial characteristics'! It seems rather that peoples are capable of the most startling reversals of behaviour within quite short periods of time. And in these years Germany was standing—as we see it now from our historical perspective—on the brink of one of these reversals.

Prussia had owed her martial prowess to the narrow cast of

Junkers whose traditions can be traced back to the warrior-knights on the Marches of the medieval *Reich*. The army they commanded had been recruited in the first place from the peasantry, who saw in their officers the feudal masters to whom they were bound 'body and soul', and secondly from mercenaries, the descendants of the *Landsknechte* of the Thirty Years War. The chief concern of the state had long been the maintenance of its great army. This the *Junkers* could not do by themselves, and the economic basis had been supplied by the manufacturers and merchants whose settlement in Prussian lands had been encouraged by the Great Elector and his successors. These new middle classes had given the state their loyalty and the struggle of the Seven Years War had revealed the existence of a Prussian patriotism.

But the political loyalty of this *bourgeoisie*, since it had no share of responsibility for the affairs of state, could not be other than provisional. Its feeling for the military was unenthusiastic; the army was a private amusement of His Majesty, and commoners were not admitted to the ranks of the officer corps. This attitude of mistrust and indifference remained typical of the *bourgeoisie* right up to 1870 and was inherited by the Social Democrats after the foundation of the Second *Reich*. Yet this is to reckon without Romanticism. It was only necessary to see in the *Junkers* the heirs of the medieval crusaders to win over the middle classes to ideals and concepts once confined to the backwoods of Brandenburg and Pomerania. At this point the Romantic Movement merges into the National Revival.

The roots of the National Revival are to be found in Berlin between 1806 and 1814, and some of them are strange indeed. A contemporary gives this description of ' *Turnvater* Jahn', the founding father of German gymnastics, who was to be alternately worshipped and ridiculed by successive generations of jingoes and anti-jingoes: 'I was taken as a child to see Jahn at his open-air gymnasium whither the youth of Berlin flocked at

Death-mask of
Frederick the
Great

'Prussia's glory . . .

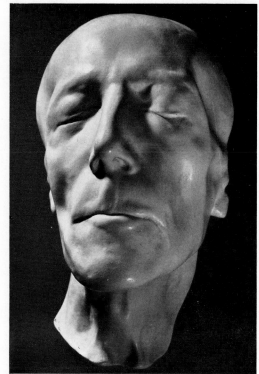

. . . and the price to be paid'

Andreas Schlüter
Head of Dying
Warrior

The Eagle triumphant: Bismarck at the Congress of Berlin 1878. Painting by Anton von Werner

(Ullstein-Hanfstaengl)

that time. In the ancient world it was an accepted thing that not only the mind but also the body ought to be trained. Now this doctrine was being preached as a novelty by Jahn and regarded with a certain raising of the eyebrows. . . . His *Turnplatz* was much frequented, partly by enthusiasts and partly by the merely curious. The gymnastic equipment on the Hasenheide near Berlin was somewhat primitive. A cleared area of a few acres in extent, screened by fir-trees, and surrounded by a moderately wide ditch, in the centre a shed for the storage of a few essential pieces of apparatus. . . . The *Turner* [athletes] had declared war on every kind of softness; only the simplest body-building food was permitted, and every sort of spirits, cakes and sweetmeats was vigorously banned. It was noticed that certain of the townspeople who had come out to watch, were sitting on the grass and devouring cakes: forthwith the whole company beyond the ditch were dubbed "the pastry-cooks". For a right-thinking *Turner* the human race could be divided into two classes: "*Turner*" and "Pastry-cooks". French expressions were avoided as much as possible by the patriotic *Turner*.'

'French expressions were avoided'—what a change from the Prussia whose greatest monarch had been pleased to converse in that language and whose German was, to say the least, faulty! But the loss of political autonomy had compelled Germans to reconsider the question: in what does nationality consist? And at once a bewildering flood of generals and philosophers, sober statesmen and inspired cranks—of whom Jahn was certainly one—had rushed forward with solutions to this problem. They were confused and often contradictory. But they had one thing in common. They tended to appeal to the past for guidance as to the future; they were Romantic and historicist. French nationalism, too, had worn the trappings of Republican Rome, but French Romantic nationalism was an anaemic thing compared with the German and the Slav variety.

There were good reasons for this. Frenchmen had long felt

themselves a political, military and economic unit; the Revolution simply rationalized what it had inherited from the *ancien régime*. But in Germany another basis of community had to be found, and it was to the glorious days of the medieval *Reich* (for Catholics) or to the days of Luther's Reformation (for Protestants) that the Romantic poets, philosophers and statesmen turned. A generation before, Herder had seen in the folksong the authentic expression of a people's nationality. And in these years two young poets of what was already the second wave of the Romantic movement were travelling the length and breadth of Germany collecting folk-songs. One of them, Achim von Arnim, was the son of a famous *Junker* clan and with his companion Clemens von Brentano, descendant of a Frankfurt patrician family, was in constant communion with the faithful in Jena and Berlin. The Grimm brothers were collecting their fairy-tales and beginning that accumulation of philological learning which was to make them the first scholars of Europe. Yet the Grimms were no dry-as-dusts. They, too, were fired by the national enthusiasm and were to pay for their patriotism after reaction had set in again after 1815. But the fieriest and most effective champion of the new spirit was the philosopher Fichte.

Fichte had something of Luther about him; Luther's massive intelligence, his rugged honesty, the mixture of professor and demagogue, and above all, the courage of his convictions. Fichte had sat at the feet of Kant in Köenigsberg and had succeeded in deducing certain propositions from Kant's teaching of which the old man would never have approved. Convinced by Kant that the pursuit of 'things in themselves' was a vain one, he had deduced that all reality must subsist in the individual ego. This radical doctrine—known to philosophy as Subjective Idealism—was a metaphysical windfall to the Jena Romantics who saw in it a deliverance from the shackles of academic Rationalism. And, indeed, this revolutionary exegesis of Kant's doctrines was a counterpart in philosophy to the

aesthetic gunpowder plot the Schlegels and their friends were
preparing.

This feeling that the individual ego must be wholly self-
sufficient in a world where all outward authority and order
have lost their validity, and must indeed *create its own world*,
this feeling is perhaps endemic in a country with a national
history like that of Germany. '*Das All und das Ich*'—the
'Cosmos and the Ego'—this is the fundamental pattern of
German mystics from Meister Eckhart to that Jacob Boehme
whom the Jena Romantics so greatly admired. But subjectivity
of so extreme a nature can never be maintained for long. The
pendulum is likely to swing back to the other extreme. Friedrich Schlegel, Brentano and Schelling sought refuge in the
Church of Rome; Novalis died young; Hölderlin, Schumann
and Nietzsche went mad; Heinrich von Kleist shot himself by
the Wannsee in Berlin in 1810 having worked out in his *Prince
of Homburg* a reconciliation of his inflamed subjectivity with
the Prussian ethic of Duty and Honour.

Fichte came to Berlin in the autumn of 1807, only a few
months after the disaster of Jena, and announced a series of
public lectures. These lectures, heavily—perhaps rather too
heavily—disguised as lectures on philosophy, are usually taken
as the beginning of the German National Movement. Reading
these *Speeches to the German Nation* now, one thinks inevitably
of the later history of this movement; a shadow is cast across
Fichte's eloquence by the hysterical demagogue who was later
to abuse his ideals. For there is no getting away from it:
Hitler's language, a hundred times brutalized and vulgarized,
is the language of Fichte. The spirits which Germany, like
Dr. Faustus, conjured from the depths in her hour of need
were to turn and rend her limb from limb. Fichte called on his
distinguished listeners in the Prussian Academy to think of
themselves as the representatives of all Germany. He reminded
them of the great works of the spirit that Europe owed to
Germany, of Luther and his Reformation above all.   The

Germans were a primeval people. They were a race whose vast potentialities were to be assumed from the undeveloped state of their physical resources and of their language as an instrument of thought. Theirs was the future: the older cultures of Europe were now nearing exhaustion.

Then, on more dangerous ground, Fichte proclaimed the philosophy of Idealism to be the German philosophy *par excellence*, and, by implication, himself to be its prophet. He pleaded for a total renewal of the system of education. Children must be taught to regard themselves as citizens of a nation and they must be as ready to live and die for it as their Teutonic ancestors had in the days of Arminius. Setting aside for a moment the consequences to which this teaching led, it is Fichte's courage that compels admiration. Berlin was still occupied by the enemy. The French had their spies and informers everywhere and it was not a moment in history when it seemed likely that patriotic courage would be rewarded. In fact, the French authorities must have considered Fichte an academic hothead and politically harmless, for no action was taken against him. But they had reckoned without the reverence with which professors are treated on the further bank of the Rhine. It was a German professor who had set the match to the pile of liberation.

The first stirrings, however, were of a reforming rather than a revolutionary nature. Baron vom Stein was requested by the King to form a ministry. The King in his distress was at last prepared to delegate power to a Prime Minister. Stein had the necessary determination and character to force through reforms that had long been necessary, and to do so against the solid phalanx of the *Junkers* of the March. But he had too much of Fichte's strong-willed personality to remain in high office for long, and within a year his ministry had succumbed to its enemies among both the *Junkers* and the French occupation authorities. His intention had been to drive out the French by using their own methods; for there were many to whom

Napoleon appeared as a liberator as he swept across Europe. By liberating the serfs, enfranchizing the middle classes and decentralizing the apparatus of government vom Stein hoped to create a Prussian, perhaps even a German, nation which should in due time rise and roll back the armies of the usurper. It is worth noting, and to the foreign eye a little comic, that this revolution was to be imposed *from above*; vom Stein, like Goerdeler the leader of the resistance movement against Hitler, thought entirely as a Prussian civil servant of the old school. Yet though his plans of reform were cut short so early, his period of office was perhaps the most fruitful until the rise of Bismarck in the 'sixties.

Something of the new spirit can be sensed in his appointment of Wilhelm von Humboldt as Minister of Education. Humboldt and his brother Alexander, the scientist, were born at Schloss Tegel near Berlin. They were at this time the most distinguished representatives of Prussian scholarship. Wilhelm von Humboldt was man of letters, political philosopher, connoisseur of the arts, and an intimate friend of Goethe and Schiller. As Prussian Ambassador in Rome he gave the rest of Europe its first glimpse of the new '*deutsche Bildung*'. He combined a profound knowledge of the classical world (he employed Schinkel to rebuild Schloss Tegel in neo-classical style) with the contemporary German passion for the ideal and the transcendental.

It is to Humboldt's initiative that Berlin owes its university, founded in 1808, and to his tact and intelligence that the young university was staffed with the most eminent scholars of the age. Niebuhr, the founder of modern historiography, teacher of Ranke; Schleiermacher, whose quaintly titled *Talks on Religion to the Cultured among its Despisers* (in Berlin, religion had to mind its manners) had an influence beyond his Romantic circle in Berlin down to the Liberal Protestantism of our day; Savigny, the great jurist and founder of the Historical Law School; and Wolff, the greatest Homeric scholar of the age,

were secured for the new foundation. The sight of so many
formidable intellects assembled in the former palace of Prince
Henry on Unter den Linden must have been imposing. It must
have suggested that what Germany could do in the realm of
the spirit ought not to be beyond her in more humdrum fields.
Once again, in authentically German terms, Theory was to
precede Practice.

The Army was in as parlous a condition as the rest of the
Prussian state. The defeat at Jena had been followed by a
collapse of morale; hardly a fortress had been defended against
the invader, the King was induced to allow even his beloved
army to be reformed. The army reformers Scharnhorst,
Gneisenau, Boyen, and Clausewitz were of the same stuff as
Fichte, vom Stein, and Humboldt. They were highly intelligent,
politically conscious men and mostly of middle-class origin.
They were widely travelled; Gneisenau, for instance, had
fought on the Loyalist side in the American War of Indepen-
dence. All were imbued with the new patriotism of the age of
the French Revolution, very different from that of the older
commanders, rugged *Junkers* like Blücher and Marwitz, who
regarded learning as 'bad for the character'. Scharnhorst was
the first of a new breed of soldier, to which Moltke later in
the century, and Beck and his friends of the 20th of July plot
also belong: the General Staff officer who was also a scholar
and scientist. Scharnhorst opened the officer corps to the
middle classes and in the Prussian General Staff created an
instrument which could outwit Napoleon—by studying and
applying his own methods.

Yet no reform or reorganization of the Prussian army could
have achieved this without the wave of patriotic enthusiasm
that spread out over Germany from the newly awakened
Berlin. The gymnastic exertions of Jahn, Fichte's exhortations,
Kleist's plays *The Battle of Arminius* [1809], *The Prince of
Homburg* [1810], and all the eloquence of the Romantics had
borne fruit. Volunteers hastened to the colours. Ernst Moritz

Arndt, Lutheran pastor and poet, summoned his master's spirit and mighty word to the cause of the Fatherland:

> Der Gott, der Eisen wachsen liess,
> Der wollte keine Knechte!

> God who caused iron to grow
> Wanted no mere slaves!

And young Theodor Körner, who with many of his literary friends in Berlin joined the volunteer brigades of the 'Lützower', wrote his famous song *Lützow's wild hunt*:

> Die wilde Jagd und die deutsche Jagd
> Auf Henkersbrut und Tyrannen!

> Wild is the hunt, the German hunt
> On the hangman's brood and the tyrants!

Körner, who fell at the battle of Leipzig, had his poems set to music by Carl Maria von Weber; his *Sword and Lyre* symbolized the aspirations of Young Germany. The shame of Napoleon's entry into Berlin had been wiped out. But not all were engulfed by patriotic emotion. Goethe had reacted to the defeat at Jena by extending a mild approval to Napoleon, his fellow Olympian who showed such a flattering interest in *Werther*. And Goethe's attitude to the Liberation was sceptical and reserved. He had long since broken with the Romantics and here was the romantic *Schwärmerei*, to which he knew his countrymen to be prone, cropping up once again in politics. Goethe disapproved; and in a new age, when it required courage to disapprove of Nationalism, he allowed his disapproval to become known.

King Frederick William III, that monosyllabic ruler, whose irresolution had been his advisers' chance and thus indirectly his country's salvation, was also known to disapprove. But royal disapproval and public disappointment belong to the following age; the '*Biedermeier*'. The period that ends in 1813 is loud with martial glory and the triumph of Romanticism.

The French troops marched out to the west and the Russians, welcome allies though somewhat embarrassing guests, marched in from the east. Berlin was free. Within a few months Paris was in the hands of the allies. The army of Frederick the Great after so shameful an eclipse had won new laurels, and Prussia acquired dominions that extended far across Germany to the Saar. Mirabeau had certainly not foreseen such a development. But then Frederick himself would have been alarmed at the fire through which the Eagle had had to go to be born again. Condemned Prussia had risen stronger than before and had become, in the Phoenix fire of Romantic enthusiasm, the potential leader of the German nation.

Chapter 5

BIEDERMEIER BERLIN

1815–1830

BIEDERMEIER is something peculiarly German, as untranslatable as the word *gemütlich* itself. *Bieder* has something of the American 'homely', something of 'pious' and something of 'worthy'; and Herr Meier is Mr. Jones. It is much to Herr Bieder-Meier's credit that the period 1815–1848 of Central European history should be named after him. For it was a period of Reaction, an Age of Disappointment between the high hopes of 1813 and the renewed revolutionary fervour of 1848. Metternich had put the princelings back on their shaky thrones with all the pomp and circumstance of the years *avant le deluge*; in the cafés of Prague, Vienna, and Berlin the political police kept their ears open for unseasonable comments. The official history of these years bristles with the titles of restored temporal and ecclesiastical worthies and their professional apologists—of whom, incidentally, Berlin supplied the supreme example in that true *Biedermann*, Professor Georg Friedrich Hegel.

It is easy to say that this attempt to bring back the eighteenth century from the dead was bound to fail. Yet the most ardent democrat cannot deny that this Age of Reaction was one of the most peaceful in the history of Europe. And it would be wrong to regard the *Biedermeier* period simply as a lull, a prelude to the next wave of idealism and violence to sweep over Europe. The *Biedermeier* period bore the fruits of peace and may be justified thereby. It saw the full ripening of the Romantic impulse in music and literature as well as the afterglow of eighteenth-century Classicism: Schubert and Schumann, Mendelssohn, Hoffmann and Eichendorff in Berlin, Stifter and Mörike and the Goethe of *Faust Part II* and *Westöstlicher Divan.*

As the predominance of music would suggest, it was *par excellence* a German period in the arts. Madame de Staël's *De l'Allemagne* had done its work; the nations of Western Europe discovered German Romanticism and acknowledged Goethe and Beethoven as their masters. At long last the culture of Germany became merged with that of Europe as a whole and even began to take the lead. This new German culture was a *bourgeois* product and was able to make a direct appeal to the middle class of surrounding nations—a class now suffering from profound political disillusionment. What more appropriate balm for Monsieur Dupont than that music with which the Germans had been lulled through centuries of princely despotism? The German praise of Nature and Solitude, the dark themes of *Sehnsucht* and *Weltschmerz*, the cult of small-town *Gemütlichkeit* and the forest idyll resounded from the keyboards in Parisian drawing-rooms and remote English country rectories. Schubert's *Lieder* and the *Tales of Hoffmann* became the property of Herr Biedermeier and his friends, however modest their circumstances. To this shaking-off of his habitual philistinism Herr Biedermeier owed the fact that an epoch is named after him.

Berlin was not, of course, the only, or even the main stronghold of *Biedermeier*. It was never, for instance, a city of music, as were Prague, Munich, and Vienna. It is curious that despite the Berliners' passion for music (and Berlin's Philharmonic and Radio Symphony orchestras are still among the best in

the world), Berlin has produced no composer of the first rank.
Nor has any composer made the city his home as Beethoven
and Brahms did Vienna or Wagner and Strauss Munich. There
is a wealth of patriotic musical legend: how Bach played for
the young Frederick at Sanssouci, how Mozart was allegedly
offered the post of Musical Director at Court but declined on
the grounds that his first duty was to 'his *Kaiser*'. There was
even a story—said to have survived no fewer than seven editions
of Brockhaus's Encyclopaedia—that Beethoven was a natural
son of Frederick the Great.

The enthusiasm of the Romantic Age for music as the most
sublime of the arts gave birth to Hoffmann's *Kapellmeister
Kreisler*. Kreisler is a fascinating creation (a forerunner perhaps of Thomas Mann's *Dr. Faustus*), the crazed musician
grasping inspiration from the jaws of madness. But for all the
fascination of the theme, and no nation has investigated so
relentlessly the diseased subjectivity of the man of genius,
there is something alien to the spirit of Berlin in morbidity and
introversion. The essential Berliner is an unrepentant extrovert.
If mysticism and music are penchants of the Germans in
general, then the Berliners are not typical Germans—indeed
they are almost Anglo-Saxon in their sceptical matter-of-fact-
ness. Thus while the culture of Vienna *was* its music, Berlin's
strength lay far more in its literature, its philosophers and historians, and in its theatre, above all in its theatre, the art *par
excellence* of the extroverted articulate Berliners.

Nevertheless even in Berlin music was the leading art of the
Biedermeier period, the period of Carl Maria von Weber and
Felix Mendelssohn. The name Mendelssohn is already familiar.
Moses Mendelssohn, the friend of Lessing and Jewish philosopher of the Enlightenment, was the first of a brilliant succession of Jewish minds down to Max Reinhardt and Walter
Rathenau to enrich the intellectual life of the city. The in-
fluential position of the Jews in Prussian society is less surprising than it seems at first sight. Prussia had been in urgent

need of a professional and commercial middle class in the early eighteenth century. The policy of religious toleration made it easier for Jews to establish themselves in Berlin than almost anywhere else in Europe. Once established, the great Jewish bankers, merchants, lawyers, and scientists became indispensable to the Prussian aristocracy. There are many examples of the *entente cordiale* existing between them: Prince Louis Ferdinand's attendance at Rahel Levin's and Henriette Herz's salons at the turn of the century, Bismarck's intellectual sparring with the Jewish Socialist Ferdinand Lassalle. Anti-Semitism in Berlin has always tended to be a *petit bourgeois* rather than aristocratic vice.

The second and most famous member of the Mendelssohn dynasty, Moses' grandson Felix, had begun to astonish the salons of Berlin as a musical *Wunderkind* shortly after 1815. Brought up among the veterans of the Romantic movement—Brentano, Hoffmann, von Arnim—who frequented his father's house, he had inherited their enthusiasms: their adoration of Shakespeare and their loving rediscovery of the German past. By the age of sixteen he had composed his music to *A Midsummer Night's Dream*. Before he was twenty he had discovered among the jealously guarded manuscripts of his master Zelter (a friend of Goethe's and a shaggy, humorous, bear-like Berliner) a copy of Bach's *St. Matthew Passion*. Bach's fame had sunk to the point where Zelter, whose word was musical law in Berlin, could refer to 'these wretched pieces' and Zelter was most unwilling to let young Felix copy the manuscript. Felix discussed his new treasure enthusiastically with his friend Ludwig Devrient, the actor, who reports how both were appalled at first by the obstacles to a performance of the oratorio. Romantic *élan*, however, finally won the day and they decided to beard Zelter in his den: 'when Zelter, who was much of a mind with Goethe on the subject of *Schwärmerei*, growled something about "a couple of young nincompoops to whom everything seems child's play"—

Felix took hold of the door handle and beckoned to me with a pale and hurt expression on his face . . . but I insisted we stay and started to argue once more.' In the end the young men got their way. Zelter gave his blessing to the great undertaking and on 11th March 1829 the *St. Matthew Passion* was presented to the modern world by Berlin's musical prodigy. In the Mendelssohn family in the Leipzigerstrasse in Berlin we glimpse a very *Biedermeier* atmosphere, the family devotion to the arts and the social life of the rich and cultured *bourgeois* in that age of aesthetic adventure and political innocence.

By contrast, the first night of Carl Maria von Weber's *Der Freischütz* was a political event—a skirmish between the 'Italian' court party with their favourite Spontini and the 'German' followers of Weber. Spontini had been discovered by Frederick William III during his stay in Paris in 1815. The King was greatly impressed by his 'Napoleonic' style—it is said that he held his conductor's baton by the middle as if he were a marshal—and the King secretly hoped Spontini's presence would endow Berlin with something of the '*gloire imperiale*'.

On every ground therefore the unfortunate man was likely to be detested by the new Romantic intelligentsia of Berlin. From the first day of his activity he was subjected to the vitriolic attacks of Berlin reviewers like Ludwig Rellstab of the old-established *Vossische Zeitung* (Berlin reviewers from Rellstab to Tucholsky have shared the Berliners' love of caustic phrase and their disrespectful candour). We have come across this preference of Prussian royalty for foreign, and particularly Italian or French, musicians and artists before. Frederick the Great's opera house on Unter den Linden was long called the 'Italian Opera'. But with the arrival of Romanticism and the more confident mood of the middle classes after the War of Liberation all this changed. The Berliners now demanded 'German music'. They wanted an opera expressing their own ideals and emotions and not the bombastic grand style of a Spontini.

Weber had written *Songs of Liberty* for the Volunteers of
1813, and his *Der Freischütz* was to be the manifesto of the new
patriotic emotions and of the new-born German arts. The day
chosen for the première of the opera was significant; the 18th
of June 1821, anniversary of the day when Blücher (or
Wellington, as you will) had won the battle of Belle-Alliance
(or Waterloo). The Opera was besieged by a vast mob of
enthusiasts—among them Heinrich Heine. At the dress rehearsal the night before, 'the technical apparatus had failed miser-
ably. In the scene in the "Wolf's Gorge" the gigantic owl had
been unable to flap its movable wings and its "blazing eyes"
had resembled rather pale street lamps.' Nevertheless the
actual performance got off to a good start. 'Weber's wife sat
in the Meyerbeer family box, near her E. T. A. Hoffmann who
contributed a number of sarcasms, young Felix Mendelssohn
and the whole Berlin intelligentsia. Uniforms were hardly to
be seen, the Court was unrepresented. . . . The appearance of
Agatha in the second act was greeted with tumultuous enthusiasm; in the "Wolf's Gorge" everything went according to plan,
the magic worked, the owl flapped its wings. The audience
abandoned itself to the enchantment of this poetry of the
German forest. That evening's victory was decisive and the
Italian party was reduced to silence.'

But victory on the stage did not mean victory in the political
arena. The aftermath of the Liberation was a humiliating disappointment to the stout burghers who had flocked to the
colours in 1813. Herr Biedermeier had hoped that his loyalty
to the Prussian throne would be rewarded by a Constitution.
But the German princes had not yet found their Bismarck, and
this outburst of patriotism on the part of their subjects caused
first embarrassment and then panic. Did not all this *Schwärmerei* for folk-songs and folk-tales and folk-lore begin to smell
of Republicanism? As though the princes of the *Reich* derived
their authority from the *Volk* and were not rulers by grace
of God? Despite the passionately monarchist and legitimist

views of many of the Romantics (Heinrich von Kleist, Adam
Müller, Achim von Arnim were members of the Christian
German Society during the Napoleonic occupation of Berlin
and their political views were essentially those of *Junker* back-
woodsmen) and in spite of their adulation of Queen Louise
and her considerably less Romantic husband, the still reigning
Frederick William III, panic spread among the aristocracy.

The unfortunate Jahn was prosecuted for subversive activity
—it was E. T. A. Hoffmann's duty as *Kammergerichtsrat* to
prepare the brief—and his famous open-air gymnasium closed.
For a couple of decades gymnastic activity was regarded by the
authorities in Prussia as inducive to High Treason. Ernst
Moritz Arndt was dismissed from his post as professor; even
Schleiermacher had to submit to police interrogation. The constitution faded into the background and the *Landwehr*, the
democratic militia that had been the pride of Clausewitz,
Scharnhorst, and Boyen, was allowed to dwindle into insignificance. The work of the Prussian reformers seemed to have
been done in vain. Even the mildest and most necessary reforms
became suspect to the King. By 1819 Boyen had been compelled
to give up the Ministry of War. In the same year, Wilhelm von
Humboldt and the diplomat Varnhagen von Ense (who fumed
against the regime in the *avant-garde* salon of his wife Rahel
Levin) resigned from the public service. All later German
historians, the nationalist Treitschke as well as the liberal
Meinecke, are agreed that this failure of nerve on the part of
the King of Prussia was a dark place in German political history. We may well agree. *Biedermeier* furniture, *Biedermeier*
portrait miniatures, *Biedermeier* poetry, and *Biedermeier* music
hardly compensate for the betrayal of the ideals of the Prussian
Reformers.

The high dreams of Novalis and his friends began to recede;
the would-be legislators of the human race remained obstin-
ately unacknowledged. Clemens Brentano who had come to
Berlin with Achim von Arnim (he later married Bettina

Brentano, Clemens's alarming sister) was followed by Friedrich Schlegel and Schelling into the womb of the church. Zacharias Werner, whose bloodthirsty dramas had once taken the Berlin stage by storm, retired to the peace of the Eternal City, there to be made priest and renounce his former productions. Others moved further and further into the world of fancy and imagination. What had been a triumphant raid on the unknown for the Jena group of friends became a shabby rout in the next generation.

Two of the stragglers of later Romanticism in Berlin were, perhaps significantly, of French origin. Adalbert von Chamisso's family were aristocratic émigrés from the Champagne, he himself had served as Prussian lieutenant and though he never mastered spoken German produced in *Peter Schlemihl* a best-seller of the period. Friedrich de la Motte-Fouqué came of an old Norman Huguenot family long settled in the March. He, too, was a Prussian officer and was decorated in the Wars of Liberation. Inspired by August Wilhelm Schlegel's lectures on German literature he gave a new impulse to Nordic Revival with his *Sigurd the Dragon-Slayer* in 1808. His *Undine* was later put to music by E. T. A. Hoffmann in 1816 and again by Lortzing, also a Berliner, in the 'forties.

But by this time the reaction had already set in. The writers of 'Young Germany' began to demand a return to the problems of the everyday world, though this movement did not get under way until after the Paris July Revolution of 1830. Yet there did not exist a clear division between the extremes, between the 'Transcendentalists' and the 'Materialists', the camp of the 'Aesthetes' and the camp of the 'Philistines', between the Ideal and the Real. The older Romantics may have had their heads in the clouds, but they knew the importance of keeping their feet firmly on the ground. About this as about everything else they had evolved a theory. Between the paradise of Art and the grey *bourgeois* world stood the Angel of Romantic Irony.

Berlin before Bismarck's Reich

1859–1959

Berlin after Hitler's Reich

Gendarmenmarkt with
the Royal Playhouse

(Ullstein-Eschen)

Unter den Linden

(Ullstein)

BRANDENBERGER TOR 1959

Schadow's Quadriga reorientated eastwards

(Ullstein-Boecker)

Romanticism is intolerable when taken quite seriously. Romanticism is an attitude, a pose. By acting a part—pious medieval knight or love-sick Hellenic youth—the Romantic calls in the old world to redress the balance of the new. By acting he hopes to change himself and the world around him. But he can never be identified with his role. In one of the earliest Romantic plays, Tieck's *Puss in Boots*, the real and the imaginary, seriousness and ridicule are mixed in the right proportions. Though the king is a fairy-tale king with a beautiful golden-haired daughter, the sharp-witted Berliners must have suspected that the author had other than fairy-tale monarchs in mind. The fairy king, for example, questions a princely wooer about his country:

> . . . In what region of our earth, prithee, may your country lie? Are you perchance a neighbour of the North Pole? Is it nigh unto the country of the savages?
>
> PRINCE: Beg pardon, Your Majesty, but my subjects are quite exceptionally tame. . . . We have as yet no reliable geography of our realms, but more is being discovered every day—it may well turn out that we are neighbours after all!
>
> KING: That would be splendid! And if there should be a couple of kingdoms in the way let me help you *discover* them. My neighbour, for instance, a good friend of mine, has a fine country—it's where currants come from—O, a delightful possession! . . . But, by the way, if you come from such a distance how can it be that you speak our language so well?
>
> PRINCE: Sh!
>
> KING: Eh, eh, what's that?
>
> PRINCE: Ssh, ssh!
>
> KING: I can't understand you!
>
> PRINCE (softly to him): Don't say that, Your Majesty, otherwise our audience will notice the Improbability of the thing.

The Berliners were delighted with the 'Improbability of the thing' and laughed hugely at the caricature of their own

F

theatrical taste and at the thrusts at the Court. This was
Romantic Irony at its best. Prussia had just taken part with
Russia and Austria in another 'profane Eucharist'—as Frederick the Great put it—after which there was no more of the
'sacred body' of the Kingdom of Poland to be *discovered* by
the three members of that unholy alliance.

Tieck's *Puss in Boots* must have inspired E. T. A. Hoffmann's *Tom-cat Murr's Views on Life*. Hoffmann was born in
Prussian Königsberg and brought with him a large share of
that *Vernunft* for which Immanuel Kant had made the city
famous. Art was for him a castle into which he could withdraw to mock at Philistia and plan petty sallies against it,
but he was the more effective because he had his own feet so
firmly on the ground. In 1816, he obtained the post of High
Court Judge in Berlin and there seems to be no doubt that
Balzac's '*conteur berlinois*' whose *grotesqueries* the French
admired so greatly was the very model of a good Prussian
official.

Hoffmann's quizzical face suggests the secret of his art.
A sharp observer of his fellow-creatures, he was unable to
take them or himself quite seriously. Behind the faces of
respectable burghers he was able to detect strangled demons
and repressed monsters. But only the artist dare reveal the true
dimensions of life—a revelation that would expose any but the
Romantic story-teller to the revenge of society. So he sat in
Lutter and Wegner's wine-shop night after night among boon
companions transformed from a Prussian civil servant (he
looked like an Italian general in his official uniform, it is said)
into a self-mocking mocker of the *bourgeoisie*. It was consistent
with his character that he should give the world his philosophy
in the form of an ostensible autobiography of a tom-cat. This
tom-cat had apparently incorporated fragments of his master's
autobiography into his own manuscript by mistake, and for
the more utter confusion of the reader, three prefaces were
provided:

Author's Preface

MODESTLY, with quaking breast, I would give the world these few leaves from my past life—Pains, Hopes and Longings which, in the Sweet hours of Leisure, have risen with Poetic Enthusiasm from my Innermost Being. Shall I, can I, be Pardoned before the harsh judgement seat of Criticism? But it is ye, ye sympathetic Souls, ye childlike Spirits, ye hearts made of the same stuff as Mine, for whom I have written. One fair tear in your eyes will be Comfort enough, and will suffice to heal the wounds, which the Coldness and Disapproval of insensitive reviewers have left on my Soul.

Berlin, May 18—
Murr, *Etudiant en belles lettres*

Foreword (suppressed by Author)

WITH the quiet Serenity which is granted to the man of Genius I give to the world my Autobiography, that it may learn how a Tom-cat can achieve Greatness; that it may learn to Recognise such excellence in its fullest degree and to offer me its Love, Respect, Honour, Admiration, and a *modicum* of Adoration.

Should anyone be rash enough to doubt the Extraordinary Merit of this remarkable book, let him Consider that he is dealing with a Tom-cat who possesses Intelligence, Wit, and very sharp Claws.

Berlin, May 18—
Murr, *Homme de lettres tres renommé*

PS. That's too bad!—Even the Author's Foreword which should have been Suppressed, has been printed!—There is nothing for it but to beg the well-disposed Reader not to bear any ill-will to the said Tom-cat on account of the perhaps somewhat over-confident tone of this Foreword. Let him bear in Mind that, were other Forewords by Certain other sensitive authors to be translated into the True Language of Feeling, the result would not be markedly Different.

—The Editor

But Romantic Irony was to prove an angel with a double-edged sword. It could be used to preserve the purity of the aesthetic paradise—and as such it was wielded by Tieck and Hoffmann in their battle with the Philistines. But it could equally well be used by the enemies of aestheticism, by those premature 'Social Realists' who wished to put art in the service of society. Thus Heine, who first visited Berlin in 1821, despite his admiration for Hoffmann's tales, reflects on the reasons for the inferiority of the German novel of society compared with the then flourishing novel of society in France and England: 'The poor German shuts himself up in his solitary attic, dreams a world together, and in a self-made language full of quirks and oddities writes novels containing people and things that are glorious, inspired, supremely poetic, but have, alas, no actual existence.' In the young Heine, who belongs to the first post-Romantic generation, we see the beginning of the reaction, the return to political and social themes that was the literary prelude to the revolution of 1848.

Chapter 6

THE BEAR'S AWAKENING

1830–1848

BEFORE we cross the watershed from the disappointed idealism of 1813 to the again hopeful idealism of 1848, something
ought to be said of Berlin Classicism. 'German Classicism'
conjures up the figures of Goethe and Schiller, the Olympians
of Weimar, attempting in their insufferably high-minded way
to live up to Winckelmann's precepts of '*edle Einfalt und stille
Grösse*'. But the cult of noble simplicity and harmonious form
was not confined to Weimar. A local Berlin bard had written
on the occasion of the completion of the Brandenburger Tor
in 1791:

> The gate of Athens hast thou, O Berlin!
> Now summon forth from cave and field
> Where they shyly are concealed
> The Muses—that they enter in!

As we have seen, it was the Romantic muse who took advantage of this invitation—though neither Prussian drill nor
Berlin scepticism can have been agreeable to her temperament. The Brandenburger Tor itself, on the other hand, has a
certain claim to the title Prussian. The admirable proportions
of Langhans' masterpiece (and of Schadow's Quadriga and
Statue of Victory on top of it) do express the Prussian passion

for discipline and order; the stark simplicity and strength suggest the rugged soldierly virtues of the March of Brandenburg. At about the same time an architectural counterpart to Wackenroder was at work in Berlin: Friedrich Gilly, son of an architect of Huguenot stock. His buildings belong to an honourable category in the history of Berlin architecture: the category of the Great Unbuilt, which includes some of the best designs of Mies van der Rohe and Walter Gropius. Gilly's plans for a national theatre and for a memorial to Frederick the Great are of an outstanding originality, reminiscent of the monumental style of French revolutionary architecture. Yet though scarcely one of Gilly's designs was carried out, his influence was immense. The sixteen-year-old Friedrich Schinkel was so impressed by the design for Frederick's monument that he decided on the spot to become an architect and study with Gilly.

The fruits of this short apprenticeship (Gilly died in 1800 still under thirty) were to give Berlin its 'Classical' profile in the 'twenties and 'thirties of the next century. In 1815 Schinkel was appointed Director of Public Works. One of his first buildings was the Neue Wache on Unter den Linden, a Neo-Hellenic venture between the heavier eighteenth-century Classicism of the University and Schlüter's baroque Armoury. But the three buildings have something in common, a something which Möller van den Bruck was to identify as 'the Prussian style', a catchword with which the young Revolutionary Conservatives of the 1920's—Ernst Jünger, Ernst von Salomon, Möller van den Bruck—made much play. But there is something distinctive, and very distinguished, about Schinkel's Neue Wache and the many other buildings with which he furnished Berlin and the March: Kreuzberg Memorial, the Museums, the Werdersche Kirche, Charlottenburg Mausoleum, and Wilhelm von Humboldt's Schloss Tegel. For the first, and last, time in her history Berlin had a unified style to express simply and with dignity her essentially Prussian qualities. To compare the boastful *nouveau-riche* mansions of Bismarck's Berlin with the 'Schinkel style' of old Berlin is to appreciate the essential modesty and reserve of 'Classical Prussia'. The term 'Prussian Classicism' is—despite its pro-tagonists—a valid one.

A little further up Unter den Linden towards the Branden-burger Tor—opposite Knobelsdorff's Opera House—stands the main University building. Founded by Wilhelm von Hum-boldt during his short term of office as Minister of Education under Baron vom Stein, it is now known as the 'Humboldt Universität'—the Eastern University to be distinguished from the Western 'Free University' in American-occupied Dahlem. On either side of its main gate Wilhelm and his brother Alexander sit enthroned, the rival champions of *Geistes-wissenschaft* and *Naturwissenschaft*—the Arts and the Sciences. After his resignation in 1819, Wilhelm had devoted his energies to the study of language; besides the chief classical and modern tongues he knew Hebrew, Sanscrit and Chinese and composed some of the first studies of them. Thanks to his original choice of teachers, the University rapidly had become the most eagerly attended in Germany, outshining within a decade the venerable faculties of Tübingen, Heidelberg, and Göttingen. Here the young Leopold von Ranke learned that methodical detective work from the classical historian Niebuhr with which he was to explode the myth-ridden history of the past. And Ranke, too, with his exquisitely balanced prose modestly concealing a megalithic learning, had something of the Prussian style—where Treitschke, leader of the so-called 'Prussian school' later in the century, was to have all too much of the overween-ing Pan-German in his make-up.

As for Science: these were the years of Helmholtz's discover-ies in Berlin, and, in applied science, the period when Borsig was laying the foundations of Berlin's engineering prowess (the Berlin–Potsdam railway opened 1838). But the Grand Master of the natural sciences was Alexander von Humboldt

himself. His travels in South America and Central Asia had
brought a vast range of natural phenomena to his attention
and provided the raw material for his *Kosmos*, a well nigh
Hegelian attempt to reduce these phenomena to one coherent
system. His charm of manner and intellectual authority gave
him the rank of elder statesman in Berlin's society at this time.
He attended Court regularly and was much lionized in the
salons of Rahel Levin and Bettina von Arnim, where Tieck still
held sway among the rapidly thinning ranks of the Romantics.

For Alexander von Humboldt belonged in a peculiar way to
the old world and the new. There was a whiff of Frederician
Rationalism about him that had been out of fashion but was
becoming acceptable again to the scientifically-minded younger
generation. His elder brother Wilhelm had remarked with misgiving on 'the new spirit' the volunteers of 1813 brought back
with them from the battlefields; 'a spirit which has contributed
much to the national life, but which has produced characters
more exclusively concerned with practical realities than those
of my own generation and that of Schiller and Goethe, who
had time to cultivate an inner, spiritual life as well'.

Friedrich Meinecke, the last great Berlin historian of the line
of Niebuhr, Ranke, and Treitschke, quotes this passage in his
German Castastrophe of 1946. He takes it as evidence of the
change that came over the German outlook on life in the years
after 1815, of a turning towards practical activity and away
from speculation. At the very moment when Herr Biedermeier and his rulers seemed to have struck a compromise—
political power for the prince, domestic peace for his subjects—
a contrary movement was getting under way; a movement of
the historical dialectic not at all to the taste of the brightest
luminary of the university, Professor Hegel.

Hegel himself was perhaps too much of a *Biedermann* to see
this or to appreciate its significance. Though certainly one of
the greatest philosophers of all time, Hegel was also very much
a child of his own. Did he not owe his honoured position as

Prussian state philosopher to elaborate proofs that, just as his philosophy was the definitive philosophy, so the Prussian state was something very like a definitive expression of the Absolute? In his *Inaugural Lecture* of 1818 he had spoken warmly of the Prussian state 'which has now gathered me to itself', and which 'owes its greatness in the world as much to its intellectual eminence as to its feats of arms'. He had spoken of the decay of philosophy in the rest of Europe: 'Science has fled to the Germans and will owe its continued existence to them. It is for us to preserve this holy flame, it is our duty to care for it and nurture it and make sure that the loftiest thing in the possession of man, the self-knowledge of his being, is not extinguished and allowed to perish.' It was a high claim—no higher had been made since the days of Plato's Academy—and it was not to remain undisputed.

Hegel's influence was immense; generations of true-blue Prussian public servants were to be reared within the hallowed walls of 'The System'. But Berlin was not the place where such an intellectual tyranny could be upheld for long, nor the Berliners the sort of people to accept the Prussian Monarchy as God's Last Word. And within a few years Schelling had begun the work of demolishing his predecessor's system from the professorial chair itself (among his audience the young Soeren Kierkegaard from Copenhagen who was to explode the whole edifice of Idealism with his savage wit). And the writers of the pre-1848 'Young German' movement—Heine, Börne and their imitators like the Berliner Karl Gutzkow—proceeded joyfully with the work of destruction.

Another of them, Gustav Kühne, gives a delightfully ironical picture of Berlin in the early 1840's: 'It was the high noon of Hegelianism in Berlin, the period when the Lord God himself—so it was rumoured—had descended to our little world of Berlin and ascertained for himself its glory and perfection. Hegel had provided proof of Monarchism, he had provided proof of Christianity, he had provided proof of our existence;

and all things existed and were very good—in so far as Professor Hegel had provided proof of them. He had proved to us that Nature was not up to much—and Lo! we looked around us in Berlin and indeed Nature was *not* up to much. So I went forth determined to glimpse for myself this temporal thing that was yet the most perfect expression of the Idea. I strolled to the great parade ground to see the military monarch who had made all this possible. And there he was, a man of steel, exemplary in carriage, glance and conduct, Absolute Justice in human form! Embodiment of Order! Idea become Reality! "What is not true—is not real: only the Truth is privileged to become Reality"—the famous proposition struck me like a rifle butt on the back of the skull. Our King had promised his people a constitution, the constitution, alas, had not become Reality, *i.e.* had not been of the Truth, for had it been of the Truth, it must unfailingly have become Reality. Just then some squadrons of cavalry approached, the band struck up a march by Spontini and I could not but join in the frantic Hurrahs that echoed round and round the parade ground.'

It was in 1836 that Karl Marx, Hegel's most famous disciple, arrived in Berlin. Like other young intellectuals of his generation he had been attracted to Berlin for its philosophy (though Hegel himself had died in 1831). Like his contemporaries the 'Young Germans', he was a rebel, a radical enemy of the *Zeitgeist* and the *status quo*. In Berlin he met the 'left Hegelians' who were busily ransacking their dead master's system for pieces they might use in their own. Hegel's methods of analysis were at a premium here, while his orthodox Lutheranism and most of his metaphysics were contemptuously thrown overboard. David Friedrich Strauss wrote his famous *Leben Jesu* (which George Eliot admired and translated), Bruno Bauer turned Jesus into a social revolutionary, while Ludwig Feuerbach went even further in transforming his master's Objective Idealism into a thoroughgoing Materialism. The young Marx must have taken part in endless beery discussions at which his fellow-students chipped away at that metaphysical colossus, like dwarfs at some stone giant. His own idea was charmingly radical in its simplicity, in his own phrase 'I stood Hegel on his head and put him the right way up.' With the fury of an Old Testament prophet he began to rage against the dreamers and word-spinners who had ruled the mind of Germany since Wackenroder and Tieck had launched their medieval *Schwärmerei* on the Berlin of the 1790's.

For Marx the prophet—as for Kierkegaard—Hegel's system was not merely false, it was evil. It was a monstrous piece of human presumption. Man had to be made to realize that his body was not the creature of his spirit as Schiller had once proclaimed, but that on the contrary his mind itself was the product of environment, of social conditions and of the struggle with Nature. Man lives by bread alone! In Marx's hysterical insistence on the forgotten basis of human life there is the authentic Old Testament note both of the religious debasement of man and of national self-castigation. On the subject of history he wrote in the *German Ideology*: 'In dealing with the Germans who boast a "historiography without presuppositions" we must begin with a presupposition that is, to be sure, the presupposition of all human existence. I mean the presupposition that men must have the wherewithal to live before they can make history. To live, however, it is necessary to eat and drink, to have a roof over one's head and clothes to wear, and certain other things. . . .' And like a true prophet Marx could tolerate no allies. In his *Theses on Feuerbach* he wrote contemptuously 'the philosophers have merely interpreted the world, but the point is how to change it'.

Marx has succeeded moderately well in changing the world; but not at all in changing his own countrymen. In furthest Viet-Nam and darkest Congo the revolutionary ideas of *Biedermeier* Berlin are seized upon as a revelation. The senior party member will gravely explain the significance of 'the negation of the negation' and 'the objective logic of history' to the listening circle in the mud hut. For Marxism is a philosophy preserved as a fly in amber. The vitriolic disputes of the founder with Feuerbach or Bakunin or Lassalle take their due place in Marxism-Leninism. Like Judaism from which it derives, Marxism is very much a historical religion. And since it was in Berlin that Marx first arrived at his revolutionary convictions (though the essential dogma 'salvation through the working class' may not have been worked out until his later exile in Paris), Berlin must always have a special significance for World Communism: a consideration which added to the drama of the blockade of Berlin in 1948. Similarly, the workers' rising of June 1953 was a doubly painful blow to Communists because Germany had always been the Promised Land of the Revolution, an opinion held not only by Marx himself, but by many long after the Soviet Revolution had been successful.

In a later chapter we shall consider the reasons for Germany's failure to live up to her revolutionary role; but the reasons for the failure of the March Revolution of 1848 in Berlin are plain enough. When Marx cursed the *bourgeoisie* he was no doubt thinking as much of the Berlin *Spiessbürger* as of the middle classes of his native Rhineland. And about the cravenness of the Berlin *bourgeois* all good revolutionaries were agreed. Marx's anarchist opponent Bakunin had written to Alexander Herzen after a visit to the city in the early 1840's: 'Berlin is a fine town, excellent music, cheap living, very passable theatre, plenty of newspapers in the cafés. . . . In a word, splendid, quite splendid—if only the Germans weren't so frightfully *bourgeois*. Yesterday I noticed a sign outside a shop: the Prussian eagle above and below a tailor ironing. And underneath the following couplet:

> Unter Deinen Flügeln
> Kann ich ruhig bügeln.
>
> Under Thy so potent wing
> I can do my ironing.'

The Eagle and the Bear! We noticed in an earlier chapter the ambiguity of the Berliner's attitude to authority—that despite his bearishness he is readier to admit the need for it than, say, the Parisian. In other words, that he is less of a revolutionary by nature. It would be as wrong to accept Bakunin's verdict as to fall too uncritically for the legend that Ernst Reuter created for his Berliners, the legend of Berlin as the bulwark of a militant and freedom-loving West. The years before 1848 were buzzing with revolutionary activity. And for the first time the voice of proletarian Berlin made itself heard. Pamphlets and lampoons began to be published in pithy dialect and the Berliner's wit received in these years a political twist which it has never since lost. Berlin's first full-blooded political satirist Adolf Glassbrenner launched from exile a dozen oblique and not-so-oblique attacks on pre-1848 Berlin— the more deadly for their lightness of tone. Squibs like the following mock-syllogisms enraged a Prussian officialdom that had lost its sense of humour since the days of Frederick the Great (who would have given as good as he got):

LOGICAL PROOFS OF THE NECESSITY FOR SERVANTS OF
THE STATE

1. *Lieutenants of the Guard*
   Were there no Lieutenants of the Guard—
   There would be no Honour;
   Were there no Honour—
   How could dishonour ever be wiped out in blood?
   If it could not be wiped out in blood—
   There would be no Challenges or Duels:
   But there are Challenges or Duels:
   Ergo—
   There must always be Lieutenants of the Guard.

2. *Nightwatchmen*
   Had there never been Nightwatchmen—
   So would Mankind never have slept;
   Had Mankind never slept—
   Germany would not be as it now is;

Were Germany not as it now is—
We would not have 40 varieties of Patriotism;
But we have 40 varieties of Patriotism—
Ergo—
There must also be Nightwatchmen.

The story of the 1848 Revolution has often been told; and
it remains, told from whatever angle, an inglorious revolution.
The Paris July Revolution of 1830 had produced not a ripple
in the placid lakes of *Biedermeier* Berlin. In literature it was not
until the death of Hegel in 1831 and Goethe in 1832 that the
spell of authority over the minds of the German intelligentsia
began to be broken. Only then did the writings of Heine, Gutzkow, Büchner, Freiligrath and other Young Germans, though
officially suppressed, begin to be widely known and discussed,
and the Parisian newspapers in the coffee-houses of Unter den
Linden become a centre of attraction.

In the 'forties, too, a new element enters the life of the city.
The capitalist world was suffering from its first great slump;
famine and cholera decimated the populations of Europe
from Ireland to the Polish provinces of Prussia. To the north-
west of the city in Moabit, a new Proletarian Berlin was growing up around the factories of Herr Borsig. Bettina von Arnim
went slumming there and brought back stories of the indes-
cribable squalor and misery in those new settlements. The so-
called 'potato rebellion' of 1847 formed a kind of rehearsal for
the battles of the following year. Housewives, infuriated at the
profiteering of the potato merchants, took the law into their
own hands and rushed the stalls. Immediately a general plunder
began and the military had to be called in to restore order.

During the early months of the following year tension grew.
On the 16th of March 1848, the news that Vienna had risen
and Metternich been compelled to flee put new heart into the
Berliners. The military were jittery; they were now more than
doubtful whether the King would have the courage to defend
his own absolutism against the Berlin *canaille*. Finally the King

granted a recall of the Diet. The grateful burghers (and, according to some authorities, 'rougher elements from the proletarian north-west') swarmed onto the Schlossplatz to pay homage to their sovereign—a last and pathetic evocation of Herr Biedermeier's faith in the good intentions of his ruler. Seeing the excited crowd approaching the Schloss, the military lost their heads. General von Prittwitz ordered the Schlossplatz to be cleared. The burghers, bewildered but in no way spoiling for a fight, were beginning to disperse when, by the pure accident appropriate to farce, a rifle was discharged. A cry of 'treachery' went up, and the King's advisers looked on in horror as the soldiers grimly cleared the Schlossplatz and the burghers fell back to build barricades, in orthodox Parisian fashion.

Farce now reigned uncontested in the once sober atmosphere of *Biedermeier* Berlin. For if the students and workmen on the barricades had little experience of such warfare, the crack regiments of the Royal Guard had even less. No manuals on street-fighting had ever been issued in Prussia; they had never been necessary. And Berlin saw the morale of the finest troops in Europe break under a hail of chimney-pots and boiling water. Before evening they had retired to the Schloss where the King was debating his next move. Caught between two fires—an ultra-royalist army and a would-be royalist people—the King decided on a Romantic gesture appropriate to his temperament. The Guard would retire to Potsdam and the People have their Constitution. As a symbol of reconciliation between monarch and people he would himself appear on the balcony of the Schloss and receive the homage of 'his beloved Berliners'. And on this strange scene the curtain goes down. For it was not the people who were paying homage to the King, but the King who was being forced symbolically to pay homage to the people. The bodies of the fallen burghers were carried onto the Schlossplatz and in response to the summons of the crowd the King bared his head. To the romantically-minded this may have seemed the longed-for reconciliation of Crown and Nation. But behind the King's back in the spacious state-rooms of the Schloss the generals glared at one another help-lessly, white at the gills, intent on revenge.

Chapter 7

THE EAGLE ASCENDANT

1848–1880

KING FREDERICK WILLIAM IV was a Romanticist; not, be it noted, a Romantic—for the Romantic movement proper had long lost its impetus by 1840, the year of his accession to the throne. Novalis, Tieck and the Schlegels had been eloquent on the subject of Christian Monarchy and the Divine Right of Kings, but they had been far from exercising any political influence. The next generation of Romantics on the other hand did play a part, and a very reactionary part, in the political life of Prussia. Adam Müller, Achim von Arnim and Heinrich von Kleist had campaigned against the Prussian reformers in their 'Christian German Society'. Von Arnim and von Kleist were names of power: the *Junkers* ought to have been gratified at this unexpected literary support. Yet Heinrich von Kleist's reconciliation with Prussianism in his *Prince of Homburg* was a purely personal one. The von Kleists were among the most hard-bitten of *Junker* families. They had supplied the King of Prussia with no fewer than twelve of his generals during the course of the eighteenth century and were to supply him with many more. But for a poet there was no room in their warrior ranks.

Yet the ideas of the 'Christian German Society' had a

delayed-action effect. The Romantics themselves had become non-political again as the upheavals of the Napoleonic period gave way to the stagnation of the *Biedermeier*. But the generation born after the turn of the century had sucked in Romanticism with its mothers' milk. *Junker* children had been brought up like the rest of Germany on Grimm's fairy-tales and Norse sagas, on Chamisso's *Peter Schlemihl* and *The Tales of Hoffmann*. The King of Prussia was no exception. His father, Frederick William III, had been as dour and tight-lipped as a Prussian officer could be, without a spark of the artistic or political genius of Frederick the Great, and lacking his humour and popular touch. Frederick William IV, on the other hand, inherited the Hohenzollern love of display rather than the Hohenzollern puritanism (qualities that seem to have been alternately dominant and recessive in the family, as Bismarck observes maliciously in his memoirs). Frederick I, the first King of Prussia, had this love of display and the last *Kaiser* had it to his undoing. It is the contrary of that earthy sense of reality which is the true nature of the people of the March of Brandenburg, whether *Junker* or peasant. And in combination with the heady notions of the nature of monarchy brought into currency by the friends of Novalis it very nearly hurried the Prussian dynasty to a premature grave.

One of the King's first and most characteristic actions was the introduction of the *Pickelhaube* into the Prussian army: the 'spiked helmet' of innumerable anti-militarist cartoons. Whatever the military value of this piece of equipment—and the army of Clausewitz and Moltke was, even without it, the most efficient in Europe—certainly it was the King's Romantic medievalism that prompted him to design it and to compel his officer corps to wear it. Byron had an ancient Greek helmet constructed for him to wear in the Greek war of liberation; now Prussian officers were to be dressed up as Teutonic Knights. Yet at this very time the eagle-eyed Moltke was writing his first minutes for the General Staff on the possible strategic value of railways (the Berlin–Potsdam railway had been opened in 1838). And in 1870 Moltke's new scientific strategy was to destroy the French armies in a matter of weeks. But Moltke, of whom Paul Valéry remarked that 'for him the true enemy was Chance', was a post-Romantic and belonged already to the modern world.

The truth is that the Prussian mind had begun to suffer from that chronic schizophrenia which after the foundation of the *Reich* in 1870 was to affect wider and wider circles of the German national consciousness. On the one hand there was an absorption in the past, a doting on the lost glories of the 'Holy Roman Empire of the German Nation'. On the other, a pace of technical and scientific progress that was rapidly outstripping Prussia's Western neighbours.

Needless to say, the officers of Frederick the Great had not thought of themselves as the descendants of Teutonic Knights (though the black-and-white Prussian colours were derived from the black cross on a white ground of the Teutonic Order). If Frederick had any use for the past it was for classical antiquity, for the world of Plutarch's heroes. For the splendours of the medieval *Reich* he cared not a rap. But then in the middle of the eighteenth century the social position of the King and his nobility was still unquestioned. It was only with the French Revolution that those in authority began to look for a new justification for their position. Thus Romanticism among the Prussians increased as the real power of the King and his *Junkers* declined. The old Prussians had been as unromantic as the Highlanders before Sir Walter Scott. By the eve of the First World War the last *Kaiser* could refer to the armed forces of the *Reich*, much to the amusement of the Berliners, as 'meine schimmernde Wehr', 'my shining suit of armour'.

Looked at from this angle Romanticism is undoubtedly a symptom of Prussian decadence. Nevertheless—and this is crucial for the history of Berlin and Germany—Romanticism did not recede in Germany as it did in France after the fall of

Louis Napoleon. It was after 1870 that its greatest triumphs
were celebrated. The movement that had begun with Tieck
and Wackenroder's pilgrimage to Nuremberg gained converts
year by year (was it coincidence that the Nazis chose Nuremberg for their annual jamborees?). And its most distinguished
royal convert, apart from Ludwig II of Bavaria, was the King
who ascended the Prussian throne in 1840.

In artistic matters the King was full of well-meaning patronage. He encouraged Schinkel, summoned Schelling and the
Grimm brothers to the University of Berlin and commissioned
the Pre-Raphaelite 'Nazarener' Peter Cornelius to paint murals
for the new cathedral. Yet his fame as a patron of the German
arts was short-lived. Schinkel died in 1842. The young men
who had responded so eagerly to Schelling's philosophy at the
turn of the century were now of a mind with Marx that 'the
philosophers had interpreted the world—the point was to
change it'. The new cathedral, planned as the largest in Protestant Europe, never rose above its foundations ('here grows
the dearest grass in Europe', mocked the Berliners), and
Cornelius' designs were never carried out. Nor did the King
have better luck with two groups of statuary, 'The Horse-
tamers', a gift from his cousin the Czar which he had erected
in front of the Schloss. The Berliners claimed they represented '*Bilder des gehemmten Fortschritts und des geförderten
Rückschritts*', 'Progress Checked and Reaction Spurred'. The
Berliners' native bearishness triumphed over the kindly, bum-
bling efforts of the King to sugar the pill of Absolutism.

Romanticism was to work wonders for the champions of
the existing order; but only when backed by real power.
During the Revolution of 1848, however, the King could not
be sure of the backing of either his royalist army (who would
admit of no compromise with Liberalism) or of the *bourgeoisie*
itself, basically royalist as it was, in its then lack of political
experience and of any physical support. On the day following
the King's salutation to the burghers killed on the barricades

he let himself be paraded through the streets wearing a cock-
ade in the national colours (the black-red-gold that became the
traditional colours of German democracy: of Weimar and today both of Bonn and of East Germany). There is no doubt
that both parties were highly satisfied with the performance.
The King imagined himself at the head of a united people; the
burghers regarded him as won for their cause. A constitution
was promised and a parliament summoned.

At the end of March the King retired to his troops at Potsdam. From this time on he began to fall under the influence of
the notorious *camarilla* of Christian-German courtiers: Leopold von Gerlach, Rauch and Edwin von Manteuffel. Manteuffel
was a romantically fierce and bearded *Junker*—a later Field-
Marshal—who had cast himself for the role of Strafford in the
conflict between King and Parliament. He was a Prussian more
at home in the dashing company of the heroes of the Seven
Years War than among the prim mathematicians of Moltke's
school. Leopold von Gerlach was of a different cast of mind.
Like many of his *Junker* contemporaries he was a strict pietist.
Pietism with its emphasis on inwardness provided a counterpart to the rigid external discipline which the Prussians imposed on their offspring and themselves. The old godless days
of Frederick at Sanssouci were forgotten. In 1870, after the
victory of Sedan, a streamer across the Brandenburger Tor
proclaimed: 'Welch eine Wendung durch Gottes Führung'
('What a change of Fortune, thanks to God's Providence').
Fifty years later it was to be 'Gott mit uns'.

Bismarck describes in his memoirs a visit to the royal party
at Potsdam in the early summer of 1848. He found to his con-
sternation that the King regarded him as a 'red reactionary'.
But Bismarck was—as he proved on later occasions—too convinced a monarchist to be dismayed at the vacillating behaviour
of one particular monarch. He promptly shaved off his beard
and took the train to Berlin to explore the situation for himself.
His observations then, and during the long and fruitless debates

in the parliament which assembled that summer in Berlin, must have convinced him of one thing: the *bourgeoisie* had no stomach for a fight. Indeed it was uncertain just what the newly elected deputies did want. There were dignified moments as when Professor Grimm rose, the white-haired veteran of both Romanticism and Liberalism and addressed the assembly with great eloquence on the universal mission of 'The German Spirit'; and less dignified moments as butcher, baker and candlestick-maker, exempt from the authority's eagle eye, went for each others' throats.

But the Revolution ended, as it had begun, in farce. On the 15th of September General Wrangel was given command of all troops in the March of Brandenburg. On the 20th, Wrangel led his troops back into Berlin through the Brandenburger Tor and held a parade on Unter den Linden; he knew his Berliners and believed in the prophylactic value of a show of force. On the 10th of November his patience—and possibly that of the burghers too—was at last exhausted. His troops surrounded the Playhouse where the parliament was sitting. Wrangel seated himself on a chair in the middle of the street with all the deliberate insolence of a Prussian *grand seigneur*. An officer of the burghers' militia appeared and declared his intention of 'defending the freedom of the people and the safety of the National Assembly', 'wir werden nur der Gewalt weichen'— 'we shall yield only to superior force'. Wrangel sat back and said in broad Berlin dialect: 'Sagt Eurer Bürjerwehr die Jewalt wäre nu da'—'Tell your militia, Force is ready for 'em', and added, taking out his watch, that the parliamentary gentlemen had fifteen minutes to leave the building, likewise the militia. And Lo! pair by pair, with carefully prepared dignity, like the animals leaving Noah's ark for the dry land, the deputies walked down the steps and disappeared into the neighbouring streets. The militia too melted away leaving behind it not a whiff of the warlike ardour of the 18th of March.

Thus did the Inglorious Revolution of 1848 come to an

end: the Eagle once more in the ascendant, the Bear more than a little shaken in his self-esteem. Yet, properly speaking, the last act of the farce was still to come. On the 30th of March 1849, just over a year after the first barricades, a sad little procession drove up to the Brandenburger Tor. The 'German National Assembly', which had been sitting for months in Frankfurt am Main discussing in a highly academic manner the future of the *Reich*, had sent a deputation to Berlin. This deputation, which included Dahlmann, the historian, and the aged Ernst Moritz Arndt, a ghost returned from the heroic days of 1813, was to offer the Imperial Crown to Frederick William IV of Prussia.

A contemporary describes the scene: 'The day had come when the deputation with its gift from Frankfurt was to arrive; and it did arrive—but how! A small crowd was gathered along Unter den Linden to watch the procession consisting of hired cabs in each of which a couple of black-frock-coated and white-cravatted gentlemen were seated. The whole affair could not have been more absurdly *bourgeois*. "What, they're goin' to make our King into a *Kaiser*!" I heard a Berlin errand-boy shouting.' The King received his would-be patrons, treated them to a sermon in his most unctuous manner and dismissed them graciously, protesting that he could not accept the great honour without the approval of his fellow-princes: thus ensuring that the idea should vanish from the public mind for two decades.

The King rejected instinctively any infringement of his Divine Right, and he had many a Strafford at his elbow to keep him to his conviction. How far the young Bismarck subscribed to this faith it is hard to say; his was a royalist heart allied to a very acute and realistic mind. He realized, as the older members of the *camarilla* probably did not, that those who attempt to stand still in politics slide back. The *status quo* had to be preserved; but since it could not be preserved intact the vital elements must be secured and the rest abandoned to the turbulent *Zeitgeist*. His problem was to convince the middle classes—as had been done in England—that their interests were bound up with those of the land-owning aristocracy and of the state itself.

It was not difficult to prove the latter. Since the 1830's Northern Germany had enjoyed the benefits of a customs union and it was becoming very obvious that the existence of three dozen principalities in Germany must hinder, for instance, the development of a unified railway system. The Liberals of '48, the Grimms and Arndts and Lassalles and Wagners, had been German nationalist in their foreign policies. They demanded a *Reich* 'as far as the German tongue resounds', as Hoffmann von Fallersleben, another of their number, put it in his '*Deutschland über alles*'. Here was Bismarck's chance. The middle classes cherished two ideals; Political Liberty and National Unity. If Bismarck could persuade them to let him realize the one ideal at the expense of the other, to unify Germany by a few cheap and spectacular victories, he might be able to check their demand for a real share of political power. In essence Bismarck was reviving the oldest of remedies for internal discontent; the originality lay in his own tactical genius. Bismarck's statesmanship was brilliant, too brilliant for the good of his nation since it required a man of genius at the helm of state. And to that extent at least Otto von Bismarck is responsible for the coming of Hitler; the Germans came to expect to be ruled by a man of genius and not by ordinary mortals.

But we have anticipated. The years immediately after 1848 were fallow years politically for Berlin. A constitution had been granted, but its powers were as yet uncertain or at least untested. The real basis of royal power, the Prussian army, had if anything increased its influence. In 1857 Frederick William IV succumbed to mental disease and was succeeded by his brother, William I of Prussia, and later first *Kaiser* of the reunified *Reich*. Within a few years of his coming to the throne this military-minded monarch was involved in a life-and-death struggle with his Liberal ministers and Parliament. His demand for a greatly increased army was unacceptable to the Liberals. They regarded the army purely as an instrument of internal repression that was furthermore solely responsible to the monarch, parliament having no say in its affairs. William I was essentially a Prussian officer of the old school, dutiful and honour-loving, but rigid in his opinions (he had had to flee from an angry mob during the revolution and take refuge in England). At the height of the conflict in September 1862 William called on Bismarck to form a ministry, almost as a gesture of despair. While Bismarck was outlining his plans for securing royal military power in the teeth of democratic opposition, the King looked gloomily out of the palace windows down Unter den Linden: 'In no time at all they'll be chopping off your head out there—and not long afterwards they'll be chopping off mine', he remarked, anticipating—wrongly as it happened—the fate of Charles I of England.

Bismarck's very appearance in public or in the National Assembly was 'received as a standing insult, a challenge to the sovereign people; the Berlin comic papers showered the feared and hated new minister with their deadliest missiles'. But a successful reactionary must have the *insouciance* of a Metternich or of a Wrangel, who had since become the adored mascot of the Berliners. And Bismarck was a Pomeranian *Junker* who did not care to hide his contempt for the city *canaille*, believing that he must win the respect of the Berliners before he could win their love. Early in May 1866, as he was walking down Unter den Linden after an audience with the King, a man fired three shots at short range into his broad retreating back. Bismarck turned, grabbed the assassin (a young sympathiser with the Austrian cause) by the wrist, handed him over to a passing company of royal guards and walked on to his ministry. The admiration of the Berliners for such *sang-froid* was as generous as their former antipathy. That evening the Wilhelmstrasse

filled with cheering crowds eager to acclaim the gallant Prime
Minister who was working for the honour and glory of Prussia.
On the 9th of May war was declared on Austria; within six
weeks Sadowa had been fought and Prussia was master of Germany. Enthusiasm knew no bounds. But it was not the least of
Bismarck's triumphs that he had won the hearts of the Berliners.

Yet the true climax was still to come. Bismarck's victories
had made Berlin potentially the most powerful city in Europe;
the seat of government of a great empire, centre of a spider's
web of military and economic power reaching from Stras-
bourg to the Baltic. The overwhelming success of the French
campaign in 1870 had been as much a German as a Prussian
triumph. The humiliations which Napoleon (not to speak of
Richelieu and Louis XIV) had imposed on Germany and on
Queen Louise, the King's own mother, had been avenged at
last. Paris lay under the Prussian guns and, in the Hall of Mirrors
at Versailles, the Princes of the *Reich* acclaimed William I as
their *Kaiser*. And it seemed as if Europe was to find its new
centre of gravity in Berlin. The Napoleonic wars had been
wound up with a Congress at Vienna, the Crimean war and the
Franco-Prussian with a Congress at Paris; it seemed inevitable
that Berlin should be the scene of the next of these periodic
stocktakings. (Who could have foreseen the apparent turning back of the clock in 1918 when the Prussians in their turn
were humiliated at Versailles? But it did not last: Russia was
absent from Versailles, the concert was incomplete. In 1945,
with Russia once again represented, the power needle swung
back to Potsdam.)

The Congress of Berlin was not only the climax of Bismarck's career, it was the proclamation of a new era. A note of
solemnity and awe was given to the assembly by the immense
age of the statesmen taking part. Lord Beaconsfield at 74 took
five days to reach the new German capital. Prince Gortshakov,
who had once patronized Bismarck in Petersburg and now

accepted his pupil's patronage with ill grace, was over 80 years old and unable to walk. Count Andrassy of Austria-Hungary proposed that the Chancellor of the new German *Reich* be invited to take the chair. The painter Anton von Werner was commissioned to record the great occasion. His picture in the monumental-academic style shows Bismarck towering like some ancient Teutonic oak over the conference table, the older powers of Europe so many sparrows under the shelter of its branches. And there was truth in this image of the Iron Chancellor as the arbiter of Europe. After the Berlin Congress of 1878 the Eastern question could be shelved for a generation, and Bismarck could spend the remaining years of office skilfully appeasing the demons that his earlier indulgence in blood and iron had conjured up. He had conquered the Berliners and the Bavarians and won back the friendship of Vienna. It seemed that even the recalcitrant French might be brought within the charmed circle of his statesmanship.

Fame quickly went to the heads of the Berliners. In 1870 the population was still under 1,000,000, by 1890 it had reached 2,000,000, and by 1914 nearly 4,000,000. A vast speculation in old property and new building began for which capital was readily available in Hamburg and Frankfurt am Main. Trade followed the flag: the new 'black-white-red' which Bismarck had planted so firmly in the sandy soil of the March of Brandenburg. These years, known as the *Gründerjahre*, 'the founding years', were aesthetically the most disastrous in the history of Berlin. Before 1870 Berlin had been a provincial city, but it had inherited many fine buildings from the eighteenth century and the age of Schinkel. Its very poverty had prevented the worst excesses of architectural revivalism.

But 1870 brought a fatal conjunction: easy money and lack of any taste or direction in matters of style. The city began to spread out with a lava-like flow away from its old centre (*i.e.* old Berlin, the area within the gates of the original city, bounded by the Oranienburger Tor to the north, the Brandenburger and Potsdamer Tor to the west, the Hallesches Tor to the south and Alexanderplatz to the east). It began to spread out into the open country, into the sandy infertile March where its flow was broken only by the old-established and now to be engulfed villages of Tempelhof, Schöneberg, Wilmersdorf and Pankow. One amoeboid arm could be seen groping south-westwards along the old highroad towards Potsdam; by the end of the century a sea of houses was about to expand from the southern rim of the Tiergarten out to Zehlendorf and Wannsee. Another arm swung along the rim of the Tiergarten due west to Wilmersdorf and Grunewald to which Society was transferring its favour. (Though many of the old Prussian families still lived in more modest circumstances in the grey Georgian terrace houses around the Gendarmenmarkt and the Friedrichstrasse.) A subordinate stream curved northwards across the old Kurfürstendamm—in 1890 still an open road where Prussian officers were to be observed taking their morning trot—to merge into old Charlottenburg. By the turn of the century nobility and *bourgeoisie* were firmly entrenched within the great triangle formed by the Tiergarten and the river Spree in the north and the Potsdamer Chaussee in the east and the Grunewald forest to the west.

But Berlin was never a city of officials and government departments as was Vienna, though a large proportion of the aristocracy who lived in Berlin did so for official reasons. Their country cousins, the *Junker* squires, preferred to work their estates in Pomerania or Silesia, where the 'Prussian virtues' had taken firmer root than in the capital with its factories and revolutions. And among the supposed enemies of the *Reich* with whom Bismarck had to contend were not only the discontented Catholics and Socialists and Polish Nationalists, but also the more conservatively-minded Prussians. William I himself was never happy with his new title of German Emperor. Prussia had stood for something—what did Germany stand for?

Yet 1870 had determined the fate of Berlin. As her Prussian
character diminished, new loyalties emerged—to the *Reich*,
and more importantly, to herself. Post-1870 Berlin has been
likened to American cities such as Chicago and San Francisco.
And the *parvenu* character of the mock-Gothic and pseudo-
Renaissance palaces in Grunewald and Nikolassee is at once
reminiscent of 'Stockbrokers' Tudor' and even 'Scottish
Baronial'. What was new in the history of Berlin was the amount
of cash available. Even the all-powerful *Junkers* had lived in
very modest circumstances and inculcated in their children the
virtues of thrift and simple living. But '*Geheimratsgotik*'—
'Privy Counsellors' Gothic'—was meant to be ostentatious.
It was a style to impress the neighbours, *nouveau-riche*, vul-
garian, American-capitalist. A quite un-Prussian intrusion.

But Berlin was not yet quite America. Despite the vast increase of population she preserved her individuality, thanks
partly to her sense of class distinction. The new officials needed
for the administration of the *Reich*, Swabians or Rhinelanders
as they might be, tended to adopt the manners of the Prussian
official class. And the same was true of the working-class in-
flux from Silesia and Saxony and from the Polish provinces.
Previously many thousands from these poorest regions of
Europe had migrated to America every year. Now, having
freedom of movement inside the new *Reich*, they tended to
come to Berlin. (The formation of a Polish Catholic proletariat is an interesting parallel with Irish Catholic immigration
to Liverpool, Boston and Glasgow.) The newcomers quickly
adopted the dialect and mentality of the older population. The
Slav blood made the Berliners, with their innate gift of the
gab, even more articulate and disrespectful of authority.

To the north and east of the city a new type of 'salubrious
dwelling for the industrious artisan' was erected: the notorious
Mietskaserne ('rent-barracks') that features in the early plays
of Arno Holz, Gerhart Hauptmann and the Naturalists. Jerry-
built, five or six storeys high, and grouped round successive

courtyards in such a way that daylight—and ground rent—
were reduced to a minimum, these *Mietskasernen* served the
needs of the new factories which were springing up. Werner
von Siemens, an artillery officer who turned to the manufacture
of electric equipment, had invented the electric telegraph and
used it for the first time between Berlin and the Frankfurt assembly in 1848. And the great engineering firm of Borsig put
Berlin in the forefront of the new Railway Age. Both firms, to
their honour, were to do much for the rehousing of their
workers at a later period. Borsig moved from Moabit out to Tegel and Siemens likewise moved out north-westwards to found
Siemensstadt on the road to Spandau. But the *Mietskasernen*
had done their work. They provided that army of the fourth
estate with which the Social Democrats were to undermine Bismarck's *Reich* long before its façade crashed in November
1918. To obtain an insight into this process we must turn to the
new literature of Naturalism that was to emerge in the 1880's.

Chapter 8

BEFORE THE FLOOD

1880–1914

THE victory of 1870 had given Germany a political centre of gravity at long last. Outside the Brandenburger Tor in the Tiergarten the column of Victory and the Reichstag arose: symbols of the new national unity and also of the means by which it had been won. It is worth considering at this point what Germany had lost through not possessing a cultural and political centre like Paris or London. The answer is surely that she had always lacked a metropolitan society. One reason why Germany had never produced a Dickens or a Balzac, a Tolstoy or a Stendhal was that she had lacked 'Society'; the local courts of the Princes had been too small and too provincial to provide a substitute for the complex civilization of Paris, Petersburg or London.

The effect had been, as Heine insisted, to drive the German writer into the isolation of his garret and his innate subjectivity. The wealth of German literature had been its lyrical poetry: the novel had remained undeveloped, the drama was strong in tragedy but weak in comedy, particularly the comedy of manners. Indeed, how was a national comedy to develop with an aristocracy that patronized exclusively the French theatre and with a middle class that had still to fight its Glorious

Revolution and lacked all confidence in itself as a class? The Princes were past masters in the game of 'divide and rule'. One does not have to be a Marxist to see in the one-sidedness of German literature a reflection of the retarded political and social development of the country.

But there was far more than a national literature at stake. The lack of a capital city with its debating clubs and political journals prevented that discharge and exchange of intellectual energy that make for the political health of a nation. Now at least there was a constitution. But it was a Bismarck constitution with a Bismarck-dominated *Reichstag*, a Bismarck-bullied *Kaiser* and Bismarck as his own foreign minister, his own deputy, exponent and executant. It was a one-man political band, the work of a superman perhaps, but one who could not delegate authority and would not retire. There was no public opinion and no public conscience: there were only temporary allies of Bismarck and the irretrievably damned 'enemies of the *Reich*'.

Very gradually as Berlin grew in power and population things began to change, until finally in the years before the First World War it became an established principle that 'what Berlin thought today, Germany would think tomorrow' (Nazism was an exception to this rule; it began in the provinces and spread to the centre). The most potent factor in this development was the rise of Social Democracy and the role of opposition to authority it inherited from the *bourgeois* parties. A single lifetime—such as that of Theodor Fontane, who regarded the change not without sympathy—had seen the transition from Absolute Monarchy in Berlin to a *Reichstag* in which the Social Democrats were the most powerful party.

Fontane had begun his literary career before '48 as a writer of ballads and established a reputation for himself as the Walter Scott of the Prussian *Junkers*. The antiquity of the fire-arm with which he had been issued prevented him from playing any very heroic part in the Revolution; and for many years he edited the famous *Kreuzzeitung* under Edwin von Manteuffel's guidance—though without sharing his reactionary convictions. He had published the delightful *Rambles in the March of Brandenburg* with its evocations of *Junker* exploits and eccentricities, whose charm is still calculated to win a modern reader's sympathy for that much derided and itself inarticulate race. Fontane, the descendant of Huguenot settlers in Neuruppin, always thought of himself as a man of the March and retained his love for the landscape and inhabitants of Brandenburg. His ballads and Adolph von Menzel's illustrations to Franz Kugler's *Life of Frederick the Great* are indeed the two best monuments to the disappearing world of Old Prussia. The personalities of both men are attractive in that they possessed certain of the real Prussian virtues, the modesty and self-irony of the Marchman and his earthy realism.

And it was this loyalty that turned Fontane in his old age into a keen critic of Berlin society. The novels he wrote from 1878 onwards are indeed the immediate forerunners of Heinrich and Thomas Mann's criticism of German society. In the opinion of Georg Lukacs the best of them, *Effi Briest*, ranks with *Madame Bovary* and *Anna Karenina* among the great realist fiction of the nineteenth century. Effi Briest is a victim of the Prussian code of honour. Her husband discovers Effi's infidelity to him many years after the event. He feels no desire for revenge and wishes secretly to forgive Effi, but he is convinced that stained honour can only be wiped clean in blood and kills Effi's lover in a duel. Effi is ruined, even the mind of her child is poisoned against her, and her father, the good-natured Herr von Briest, refuses to receive her under his roof. But the husband suffers no less. He is conscious that he has sacrificed his happiness to a 'bloodless abstraction'. Yet he is bound by the narrow social conventions of the Prussian nobility and is unable to transcend them and forgive Effi. Here the ideal of honour which Lessing had gently mocked in *Minna von*

H

Barnhelm has become the social Moloch to which the happiness of three human beings is offered up. Fontane, who had devoted his early years to the Romantic evocation of old Prussia, had become in his old age a social critic of the stamp of Zola and Ibsen.

And Berlin, too, had come of age. Hoffmann's Berlin was still a provincial town; the Berlin of Fontane's last years was already a *Weltstadt*, a metropolis. And this bustling new city with its parade grounds, its *Mietskasernen*, and its palatial neo-Florentine banking houses demanded a new literature. The years after 1870 had been lean years for the arts in Germany. Only at Wagner's Bayreuth did the new *Reich* find any sort of aesthetic expression; the muses appeared to shun the shambling, loud-mouthed, Yankee-like capital of the *Reich*. But it was not merely that pale third-generation Romanticism was incompatible with the go-getting worldliness of Berlin, the literary language was itself a debased currency. Arno Holz, who had come to Berlin from Königsberg in East Prussia as a young man, wrote in 1866 in his *Buch der Zeit, Lieder eines Modernen*:

> The German language was once in former ages
> A flaxen Maenad raging through the forests;
>   But today her former so passionate bosom
>   's flat as an ironing-board.
>
> The good little lady has drunk too much tea
> And suffers from coughs and a certain hoarseness:
>   And I question—when will she be again
>   Full-blooded and coarse like Luther?

Luther had made it his habit—as every German schoolboy knew—'dem Volk aufs Maul zu schauen', to take his German from the market-place. Holz and his generation were convinced that they must do the like if the German language was not to die of anaemia. In *Papa Hamlet*, therefore, Holz described according to his formula of 'thoroughgoing Naturalism' a microscopically observed slice of life in a Berlin *Mietskaserne*. The milieu is the famous 'Miljöh' of Heinrich Zille, the people's painter of working-class Berlin at a slightly later period. Everything is recorded with scientific precision: not a shade, not a movement, not a sound is missing. The book came out under the pseudonym Björne P. Holman, no doubt because of the popularization of Scandinavian Realism by the newly founded publishing house of Samuel Fischer who was to do more than any man to support the Berlin *avant-garde* of the Naturalist generation.

And it was not by chance that these young men came to Berlin to write. Here they found all the fauna and flora of a fast-developing modern city, Sinclair Lewis's Chicago and Zola's Paris in one. But it was not only in search of material that writers from all parts of Germany began to settle in Berlin; Berlin had become a clearing-house of European ideas. The Scandinavians were first discovered here, Jacobsen, Kierkegaard and later Hamsun; and here Ibsen and Strindberg were introduced to the European stage. Things Russian had long been popular in Berlin; Samuel Fischer, like Bismarck, had his private wire to Petersburg and was one of the first publishers in Europe to bring out editions of Tolstoy and Dostoevsky. In 1894 he had brought out the poems of the Polish modernist Przybyzewski (made fun of by Arno Holz in his play *Sozial-aristokraten*) with illustrations by the Norwegian painter Edvard Munch, also living in Berlin at this time. Even the Viennese *avant-garde*—Schnitzler, Hermann Bahr, and the young Hugo von Hofmannsthal—first appeared under the aegis of S. Fischer of Berlin who also published the first translations of D'Annuncio and Maeterlinck and the productions of the rival literary capital beyond the Rhine.

Samuel Fischer may be said to have put the German *avant-garde* on its feet. The days of the dimly-lit garret and of the royal Prussian censor were past. In 1889 the adventurous young Jewish publisher planned a two-pronged assault on

Philistia—he founded *Die Freie Bühne*, a society for the private performance of new plays, and simultaneously a weekly journal of literature. Jehovah had heard the cry of his Faithful.

On 20th of October 1889 *Vor Sonnenaufgang* (*Before Sunrise*) by the then young and unknown Gerhart Hauptmann was given its sensational and historic first night. Like many a literary *succès de scandale* the play surprises now by its tameness. But at the time it seemed the last word in Ibsenism. At one point a doctor emerges from an off-stage maternity bed gesticulating wildly with a pair of obstetrical forceps. The scene was laid among a family of hereditary alcoholics in the squalor of a Silesian mining village. The idealistic young Socialist, no doubt Hauptmann himself, who comes to investigate conditions in the village, first falls in love with the daughter of the house, then leaves her—with a homily on the genetic effects of dipsomania—to a melodramatic off-stage suicide.

It is not the 'Ibsenizing' tendency of this play which is remarkable but rather Hauptmann's great gift of observation and ability to create human character. The old Theodor Fontane, whose theatre criticism during these years made him a champion of the *avant-garde*, welcomed the young playwright and proclaimed that he had in him the dramatic force needed to shake the German theatre from its Classicist torpor. This force and the linguistic fruits of *dem Volk aufs Maul schauen* were put to their best advantage in Hauptmann's masterpiece *Die Weber* (*The Weavers*), performed by the *Freie Bühne* in 1892. This piece is possibly the best of German Naturalist plays, convincing alike in its employment of Silesian dialect and in its social compassion (Hauptmann's grandfather had taken part in the Silesian weavers' rebellion of the 'forties). Hauptmann's later plays tended to move away from Naturalism proper and become bogged down in that other Silesian speciality: Mysticism, but Mysticism with none of the fervour and precision of Jacob Boehme and Angelus Silesius. An exception is *Der*

Biberpelz (*The Beaver Coat*), which introduces Berlin dialect to the stage, and in Mutter Wolfen a *Berlinerin* capable any day of outwitting the pompous Prussian magistrate von Werhahn. *The Beaver Coat* is in the direct line of German comedy from Lessing's *Minna von Barnhelm* and von Kleist's *The Broken Jug*, to Zuckmayer's *Captain of Cöpenick*. In it Hauptmann is carrying on the plebeian tradition of Glassbrenner in the 1840's.

In a later play Hauptmann gives a social panorama of the city where he lived for a great part of his life. In *Die Ratten* (*The Rats*), first produced in 1912, he contrives to bring together in a shabby rat-infested Berlin *Mietskaserne* Herr Hassenreuter, a retired ultra-patriotic theatrical manager, his wife and daughter and a motley assortment of Berlin types. There is Herr John, the good-natured bear-like working-class Berliner; Frau John, his wife, a second Mutter Wolfen who kills herself when her husband finds out that the child she has secretly adopted is not their own; a Polish servant-girl seduced and abandoned by a guards officer, and her murderer, Frau John's brother, a vicious creature from Berlin's *lumpenproletariat*. Inevitably, Hauptmann is there too in the ironical portrait of the naïve and earnest young Spitta, former student of theology and detached observer of the life of his time.

Spitta is taking lessons in acting with Hassenreuter who sets him to recite a passage of Schiller. He does so, but in his natural voice and without the required Classical *pathos*. Hassenreuter is profoundly shocked at this mishandling of the German Classics. But Spitta tells him with youthful recklessness that 'he has thrown up theology for the same reason— because he couldn't stand the parsonical voice any more'. Hassenreuter boils over: 'So you maintain that a Berlin charwoman might in certain circumstances be as appropriate a subject of tragic art as King Lear or Lady Macbeth?' Spitta bursts out (in the spirit of the young Hauptmann): 'Before Art, as before the Law, all men are equal, Herr Direktor!' And bold with conviction he proceeds to demolish those precepts of

Weimarian Classicism which to Hassenreuter are the Alpha and Omega of dramatic art.

Spitta pleads for a return to the young Schiller, to the Goethe of *Götz von Berlichingen* and to that first lawgiver of the German theatre, Gotthold Ephraim Lessing. But Hassenreuter is not to be appeased with these august names. It is not merely the German theatre that is at stake; it is the existence of the *Reich* itself. 'You're just a symptom. Don't think you're so important. You're a rat—and you rats are starting to undermine our glorious unified German *Reich*. . . . You want to rob us of the fruits of our efforts! A plague of rats in the garden of German art, gnawing at the roots of the tree of Idealism. . . . You want to drag down the Imperial crown in the dust. I tell you! Yes, in the dust, in the dust. . . .' Then Hassenreuter breaks off, seeing Frau John coming down the stairs: 'And there's your tragic muse, young Spitta.' The point is driven relentlessly home. Frau John takes her own life, a victim of her own folly and of the squalor in which her class is condemned to live. Frau John, the Berlin charwoman, is Hauptmann's new tragic muse. The moral is plain. Neither in politics nor in the drama are the traditional forms adequate to the realities of the new century.

By 1912 the 'young *Kaiser*'—William II, the grandson of Bismarck's William I—had been on the throne for twenty-four years. Berlin had now a population of over 3,000,000 and the ruling circles of Bismarck's *Reich* seemed outwardly very well content with their place in the sun. But the year 1890 that had inaugurated a new literary and social movement in Germany, had brought in other ways a return to the Romanticism of Frederick William IV. The young *Kaiser*, who had in 1888 ascended the throne on the death of his father, the liberal Frederick III (who so unfortunately died within a few months of his accession) longed to make a splendid gesture in the manner of Frederick William IV. And no gesture lay readier to hand than the achievement of social peace in the *Reich* by 'dropping the pilot'. The aged Bismarck was to be thrown to the ostensibly wild—though in reality very tame—beast of Social Democracy.

In his autobiography Bismarck inserted by way of revenge a vitriolic little chapter on Kaiser William II. He shows the reigning monarch to be a disastrous amalgam of the unhappier characteristics of his ancestors. William II is said to have 'the love of outward show of the first King of Prussia with all his passion for dressing up and his lively appetite for flattery'. He has the autocratic leanings of Frederick the Great and the Soldier King, their desire to have the direction of all matters of state in their personal control. 'But'—Bismarck hints broadly—'while Frederick's abilities were far greater than those of any ministers available to him, can the same be asserted of the reigning monarch?'

Bismarck wickedly alleges genetic resemblances between Frederick William II and William II. He hints at a pathological sexual development and a susceptibility to mystical influences. With Frederick William III he finds nothing in common: 'That King having been silent, modest and averse to public demonstrations of affection for his person.' With Frederick William IV, on the other hand, he notes all too great a similarity. Bismarck remarks shrewdly that the Germans are more prone than other peoples to sin against the principle 'Le mieux est l'ennemi du bien.' In this and in a further point he sees the roots of their monarchs' bad government. 'They seem to believe that kings are better informed as to the will of the Almighty than other men and are able to demand of their subjects unqualified obedience without the necessity of discussing with them, or even announcing to them, their mysterious resolutions.' This was not Bismarck's idea of monarchical government. He spent his remaining years, not without a certain *Schadenfreude*, watching the ship of state veering from one tack to another, making enemies and losing friends, and drifting ever nearer to that encirclement which had been a Prussian nightmare from the time of Frederick the Great.

Needless to say the splendid gesture was of no avail. Neither the bombast of Frederick William IV at the time of the March Revolution nor William II's attempt to put himself at the head of a movement of social reform came to grips with the real problems of the age. And in William's case his patronage of Pastor Stöcker's anti-semitic Christian Social movement brought him little sympathy from either right or left. Under Bebel and Liebknecht the Social Democratic movement had become, in spite of Bismarck's anti-Socialist legislation, the most powerful in Europe. Berlin had become 'Red Berlin', feared and disliked now in the provinces as much for her class-conscious proletariat and sceptical inquiring spirit as for the dead hand of her bureaucracy and the arrogance of her guards officers.

All Germany had delighted in the triumph of the Captain of Cöpenick, the rascally (or perhaps merely simple-minded) tramp who bought a cast-off Prussian captain's uniform and proceeded to demonstrate to the world its power over the bureaucratic mind. Dressed in his Prussian blue he commands a squad of guardsmen to place the burgomaster of Cöpenick, an eastern suburb of Berlin, under arrest. No question of written authority or a warrant: the *Kaiser*'s uniform is sufficient! And it proves to be so. The burgomaster allows himself to be led away and Herr Wilhelm Voigt has free run of the municipal cash-box (Carl Zuckmayer's farce of 1928 erected, incidentally, a fitting monument to this hero of modern Berlin). Ridicule and irony had long been the Bear's defence against the all-powerful Eagle. And ridicule was the only antidote to the Romantic nationalism with which Bismarck had infected the Hassenreuters and their like. But by 1914 the rats had gnawed Bismarck's edifice hollow and not even William II's last great gesture—the last the Hohenzollerns were ever to make—could delay its fall.

On the 1st of August, the day war was declared, the *Kaiser* addressed a message to the nation in which occurred the famous words: 'From today I do not recognize parties; I recognize only Germans.' And for a few weeks the whole nation seemed ready to answer this challenge. Whole classes of students and schoolboys volunteered for the front. The Café Paris was renamed Café Vaterland. And, as to Rupert Brooke in England, the world seemed for a moment to have been born anew. In both England and Germany there is something infinitely pathetic about that mood of August 1914; but for the Hohenzollerns it was the last flash of glory. The Hohenzollern Eagle reached its zenith in 'the August days'. What came afterwards, the narrowness and folly of Hindenburg and Ludendorff, their refusal to negotiate, their provocation of America, then the slow drift to disaster and the *Kaiser*'s precipitate flight to Holland in November 1918; these things were a pitiful and undignified postscript.

Chapter 9

'THE TWENTIES'

1910–1933

'THE TWENTIES' were Berlin's Golden Age. As a rule Berliners are not given to nostalgia and are Yankee enough to think the present a little bigger and better than the past. But they make an exception of 'the Twenties'—the period that begins for our purposes about 1910 and ends very abruptly on the night of the 30th of January 1933. The sudden break is significant. The Twenties were a period of violence, a Renaissance age of gangsters and aesthetes, Savonarolas, Cellinis and Borgias. Germany in the Twenties was almost as creatively anarchic as Italy in the Quattrocento. And, despite the violence, the Berliners cherish the memories of that extraordinary decade.

The arts flourished on German soil in the Twenties as they had not since the age of Goethe. In Weimar Gropius founded his legendary *Bauhaus* with Mies van der Rohe, Kandinsky, Paul Klee, and Moholy Nagy. Einstein and Max Planck were at work in Berlin, where Relativity in the world of Physics seemed to find an echo in the despondent relativity of other disciplines and soon enough in public and private morals. What is freedom to the artist may seem licence to the *bourgeois*—but the artists certainly made the most of their short-lived freedom. The Twenties saw the great age of the silent film in Berlin: *The Cabinet of Dr. Caligari, Faust, The Student of Prague*; and the short spectacular triumph of Expressionism in literature, music, and painting.

It is often said that the German Twenties owed much to the French *avant-garde*: but it was by no means only a one-way process. There was a constant westward drift of artists and writers during these years. Refugees poured into Berlin from Russia after the Revolution and were compelled to continue their trek in the company of the largely Jewish-led Berlin *avant-garde* to Paris, London and New York after Hitler's rise to power. Dadaism began in Zürich and Berlin; a painter like Max Ernst was hailed as a 'Surrealist' on migrating to Paris in 1923. But the Expressionists proper—Gottfried Benn and Ernst Toller, the 'Brücke' painters and film producers like Murnau and Fritz Lang—were German by inspiration and by birth. And the movement as a whole was a 'Northern' one, deriving from Van Gogh and Strindberg and Edvard Munch (the last two of whom had lived for long periods in Berlin). Indeed, Expressionism sometimes resembled an incursion of the '*furor Teutonicus*' into the arts, its violence and its intensity being a reflection of the feverish sickness of German society at the time. It would be unwise to draw any conclusions from this state of affairs. Art no more thrives on violence than does any other human activity. The violence of Hitler's thugs rid Germany of the arts for a generation. But there is still reason for the Berliners, and not only the Berliners, to be nostalgic about 'the Twenties'. European history since 1914 may have been a record of ceaseless violence, but at least in Twenties Berlin it was violence-cum-creativity.

There is another reason for the nostalgia of present-day Berliners. The Germany of the Twenties is unthinkable without Berlin (whereas, today, there is the ever-present fear that Berlin may come to be 'expendable' to the strategists). Not that Berlin was universally popular. There was little love lost

between *parvenu* Berlin and the ancient cities of the *Reich*:
Munich, Hamburg, Frankfurt am Main, each with its claim to
hegemony in art, trade and finance. To South Germans Berlin
was still the capital of Prussia and all the diplomatic skill of
Bismarck could not eliminate the simmering resentment against
the *Saupreussen*: half indignation at Prussian arrogance and
half envy of the superior energy and efficiency of the North
Germans. This complex of jealousies and aversions was as
potent after as before the First World War (and incidentally
shows little sign of exhaustion today). Yet by the end of the
First World War the instinctive distrust of Berlin had under-
gone a change. Looking to the north the South German *bourgeois* began to see not Prussian-true-blue but Spartacus-red.

Berlin was the city of Revolution and of all kinds of immorality. It was the city where Ernst Toller, Bertolt Brecht and
their friends had continued to flourish after their extremely
amateurish revolution in Munich had collapsed. Adolf Hitler
had been the man to reap the fruits of this piece of literary
politics and of the pent-up resentments of 'under-privileged'
Bavaria when he proclaimed his march on Berlin in November
1923. On this occasion, however, as during the Spartacist
rising of January 1919, the central government succeeded in
asserting its authority. Hitler's revolt as well as the would-be
German Communist Revolution of the Spartacists had been
nipped in the bud by an alliance between the Social Democrats
and the defeated *Reichswehr*. On both occasions Berlin was
saved the fate of Paris in 1871, the fate of a revolutionary capital
surrounded and dragged down by reactionary provinces.

But the defeat of Hitler in 1923 was only a temporary
triumph. The forces he represented were to prove too strong
for Berlin; the Republic and its Republican capital were to
prove a head without a body. Hitler was the mouthpiece of the
little men from the provinces who, confused by the democratic
hubbub of Berlin, still looked for guidance to those Prussian
upper classes who had no longer the will nor the power to

determine the fortunes of the *Reich*. The irony of the situation was that the Prussification of Germany had succeeded all too well. Every provincial schoolmaster had become a little Treitschke, an eulogist of the tradition of the Great Elector, Frederick the Great and the Iron Chancellor. Hitler himself, though an Austrian, had a naïve admiration of those godlike beings, the gentlemen of the Prussian General Staff—an admiration to vanish after later contact with those Immortals.

The *Junkers* had followed their *Kaiser* into voluntary political exile. They retired to their country estates in Pomerania and East Prussia where they occupied themselves with hunting, shooting and fishing until better days should return. And their absence from the political scene was Hitler's chance. He had only to mobilize the little men from the provinces and to impose their will on the vacillating centre. The German people, who had been accustomed to receiving orders from Berlin in the past, longed to receive orders again from an authoritarian centre. Hitler did not succeed in marching on Berlin in 1923 as Mussolini had marched on Rome; but organization was to succeed where force had failed. Red Berlin was not taken by storm; it was swallowed whole by the provinces.

But the hour of the 'Great Expressionist' was still to come; in 1910 Hitler had just arrived in Vienna seeking an outlet for his artistic gifts in socially acceptable ways. But artistically Vienna had already lost her supremacy to Berlin in the years before the First World War. Even the Berlin world of painting was sharing in the general aesthetic ferment. Into the neatly ordered Naturalism of Berlin academic painting about 1910, burst the ecstatic visionary works of the 'Brücke' group from Dresden; Kirchner, Otto Mueller, Schmitt-Rottluff, Nolde and Pechstein. Berlin was becoming a capital of modern art. Yet it is doubtful how far one can speak of a 'Berlin tradition' in painting any more than in music. The city has never had an artists' colony to compare with Munich's Schwabing or Paris's Montmartre.

Realistic scenes from family and small-town life had been very popular in the past, together with the variety of Classicism favoured by Schinkel and Wilhelm von Humboldt. And there had always been one or two painters and sculptors in each generation to satisfy these tastes. In the late eighteenth century Chodowiecki from Danzig, 'the Hogarth of Berlin', had recorded the social life of the Prussian capital with great charm and skill as an engraver. Zelter's contemporaries Gottfried Schadow and Christian Rauch were the two representative figures of *Biedermeier* Berlin. Rauch's *Entry of Blücher into Berlin*, in imitation of the Parthenon Freeze, was greatly admired in its generation. Goethe even had a copy made for his house in Weimar. And Schadow, a bear of a man after the heart of the Berliners, had designed the Quadriga of the Brandenburger Tor and carried on the tradition of Chodowiecki in his caricatures of Berliner fashions and follies. Caricature, indeed, had always been to the taste of the Berliners. Glassbrenner's political satires in the 1840's had appeared with illustrations by Theodor Hosemann in the style of Cruikshank. The later 'Kladderadatsch', the Prussian counterpart of *Punch*, kept up a constant fire at the 'Borussianism' of the swarms of little would-be Moltkes and Bismarcks. And the culmination of all these assaults on the Prussian Establishment was to come in the Twenties with George Grosz's savage studies of the Berlin *petits bourgeois* and the 'hard-faced men who did well out of the war' in his famous *Das neue Gesicht der herrschenden Klasse* (*The New Face of the Ruling Class*).

That ruling class itself had done little to preserve its features for posterity, though the *Junkers* sat stolidly for their portraits to Franz Krueger in the 1830's and again to the great Max Liebermann round the turn of the century. Such glory as 'Borussianism' attained in the arts it owes almost exclusively to Adolph von Menzel. Menzel's Frederick the Great—as he emerges from the illustrations to Kugler's *Life*—is an altogether more sympathetic character than the Hero of Carlyle.

And Menzel himself was a great Berlin character, physically not unlike Frederick. Jules Laforgue, who was French reader to the Empress Auguste in the 1880's, described his gnome-like figure 'haut comme une botte de garde cuirassier, chamarré de colliers et d'ordres', hurrying among the distinguished personages of the court, knowing everybody—'le terrible Menzel, le plus enfant terrible des historiographes'. It is, indeed, strange that Menzel has remained practically unknown outside Germany. Laforgue commented on his *Coronation of the King at Königsberg:* 'interessant essai de realisme et même d'Impressionisme dans un tableau officiel'. And Laforgue —fresh from the Paris of the Impressionist Age—would not have used the term lightly. In many ways Menzel anticipated Impressionist technique, though rather in his town-scapes of Berlin than in his official court paintings.

Impressionism proper emerges towards the end of the century and is more frankly dependent on the Parisian school. Nevertheless Max Liebermann ranks with Sickert as a non-French interpreter of the style and Max Slevogt and Lovis Corinth not far below him. Max Liebermann, notwithstanding his Jewish descent, became a pillar of Prussian respectability and no villa of the *haut-bourgeoisie* in Grunewald or Nico-lassee was complete without a portrait by him or a landscape by Corinth or Leistikow. Proletarian Berlin too had its champion in the much-loved Heinrich Zille, himself a proletarian who, self-taught and not jealous of public honour, spent his life recording the squalor and humour (often extremely rough humour) of the inhabitants of Wedding and Moabit. A delightful drawing which he made as a birthday present for Max Liebermann introduces the ragged-trousered and scruffy-haired world 'over the river' to the benevolent doyen of Berlin artists standing at the door of his house on Unter den Linden. It is a confrontation like that of Hassenreuter and Frau John in Gerhart Hauptmann's *Die Ratten.*

But Art cannot afford to be respectable for long. And

Liebermann himself had supported the breakaway from the old Academy in 1899 to found the 'Berliner Sezession' that first exhibited the works of Gauguin and Van Gogh. At a session of its hanging committee about 1910 someone is said to have asked about a picture of Kirchner's: 'Are you going to call this Impressionism too?' To which, legend has it, came the reply: 'Well, scarcely, it's rather Expressionism!' And this group of young painters from Dresden had indeed broken with the traditions of Menzel's and Liebermann's painting which, if not technically daring, had appealed to Berlin and its practical middle-class taste.

Like the Romantics a hundred years before, the 'Brücke' painters were all North Germans. They were not born into any tradition of the visual arts and were therefore thrown back on their subjectivity; which was both their strength and their weakness. The weakness only became evident later as the vision faded, the vision that had succeeded for a moment in transfiguring the monotony of the North German landscape and the stylistic tohubohu of Berlin's architecture. The 'Brücke' painters have been called 'the German Fauves', and they had the same revolutionary palette and boldness of line. But they lacked the intellectual substance which enabled Rouault or Matisse to develop further. The fault lay—at a guess—with the exaggerated subjectivity. Yet the paintings that Kirchner, Pechstein and Emil Nolde produced in Berlin both before and after the First World War (together with the 'Blauer Reiter' group in Munich) gave a new impulse to European art. The years before 1914 in Berlin witnessed in fact the rebirth of German Romanticism in a movement which was soon to embrace not only painting, but poetry and music, the stage and the screen as well.

Expressionism was a cry from the heart; it would be foolish to reduce it to a system. It was a protest—a protest against war and the society that had given birth to war. But strict chronology is liable to mislead: the most memorable expres-

sionist war-poem was written before the war itself by Georg
Heym, who was drowned while skating on the Wannsee in
1912. It is often suggested that Heym's *Der Krieg* was a prophetic vision of the coming slaughter. But it was perhaps something more than that: a vision of human evil, demonically
personified, stalking through the great cities of the West long
before the actual outbreak of hostilities:

> Resurrected is he from ancient sleep,
> Risen once more from the vaulted deep,
> Tall and unknown in the twilight he stands
> And he pulps the moon in his two black hands.
>
> For through the cities' evening noises wade
> The stranger's dark presence and his frosty shade—
> And all the whirling markets stiffen to ice.
> All's quiet. Each looks around and no man knows.

The giant dances on the mountains, calling on his warriors
to join in the frenzy of destruction; he drives fiery death before
him into the night like 'a red hound baying':

> And the flames rage hungry from wood to wood
> Like yellow bats, zigzag in search of food.
> He crashes his mighty club into the blaze
> Splitting the tree-trunks that the fire graze.
>
> A city went under in that yellow smoke
> Jumped into the abyss and never spoke . . .
> But giant-like above the glowing ruins
> He stands who thrice his bright torch turns
>
> Above the ragged clouds' storm-scattered light
> Towards the icy wilderness of the night
> And sets the darkness blazing like a witch
> Above Gomorrah's sea of burning pitch.

The poem has no doubt the faults of Expressionist poetry
in general. Its lurid colours are those the 'Brücke' painters
employed on their canvasses and the startling imagery may disguise the conventionality in other respects—in the metre, for

I

example. Here Eliot, Pound and the Imagists, Heym's contemporaries in England and America, were far more revolutionary. Expressionism was perhaps more important for its
historical witness than for its actual literary achievement. But
this would be unfair to the new generation coming to maturity
about 1910. They were not interested in art for its own sake.
They were men possessed, consumed by a certain vision of the
world which had at all costs to be got on to paper or canvas.
And they had a sense that time was short. It was in these years
that Oswald Spengler began work on his *Decline of the West*
which was to make such a stir in Germany after its publication
in 1919. For those in Central Europe with eyes to see and ears
to hear the atmosphere was tense with conflict and foreboding.

Yet in what did their vision consist? Was it merely a horrific
social and political apocalypse—an apocalypse, as in Heym's
poem, with a demon rather than a saviour? It is tempting to
read *Der Krieg* in this way. There is an uncanny element of
Schadenfreude in it over the destruction of Gomorrah-Berlin
(the Expressionists' vision was to become lurid reality in the
thousand-bomber raids of the Second World War). Its Nihilism is echoed in Gottfried Benn's famous *Morgue* of the same
year, 1912:

> The solitary molar of a prostitute
> Whose death passed unmentioned
> Has a gold cap to it,
> The others have left as though by
> Tacit agreement.
> Then the morgue assistant knocks this one out,
> Puts it in his pocket
> And goes dancing.
> 'For,' says he
> 'Dust, only dust, shall return to dust.'

Reading these poems of pre-First-World-War Berlin one
wonders what Western intellectuals had to learn from 'La
Nausée' and the anguished pessimism of post-Second-World-
War Paris.

Berlin's Americanism and the breakneck pace of her expansion—she had grown from under 1,000,000 in 1870 to
nearly 4,000,000 by 1914—gave her a quality which other
European cities lacked. There existed, on the one hand, a
restless and uninhibited search for new forms; on the other
the manic depression of megalopolitan existence. Hysteria is
evident in the rapid fluctuation between optimism and pessimism, and in their cohabitation. Right up to the war and even
during the recurrent economic crises of the Twenties Berlin
was an expanding city. It was a city both of unlimited opportunity and of high unemployment. Vast fortunes were to be
made and lost on the stock-market, and Berliners of all classes
were (as Treitschke noted sternly in the 1880's) inveterate
gamblers.

Berlin was a second Chicago. Her jungle atmosphere is unmistakable in Döblin's novel *Berlin Alexanderplatz* and in the
plays of Bertolt Brecht. Berlin is the real background to the
majority of the plays of Expressionism. In these the latent hysteria found its literary expression; though the intensity of the
protest or the human agony was often too much for the loosely
strung scenes to bear. There seems to have been a general urge
towards the drama; almost every young writer had a play to his
credit. And not only the writers. Oskar Kokoschka, the
painter, wrote his first play in 1910 and designed settings for it.
Ernst Barlach, the sculptor, produced a series of religious
plays much discussed at the time in Berlin (his last play *The
Count of Ratzeburg* was written under the Nazis and is among
the most moving and original of modern Christian dramas).
Even Gottfried Benn wrote a play, like his fellow-Expressionists Else Lasker-Schüler, who added an exotically Jewish
element to the writing of her masculine contemporaries, and
Johannes R. Becher, later to preside over culture in Communist East Germany. And of the dramatists proper there were
Georg Kaiser, most brilliant and productive of them all,
Walter Hasenclever, Arnolt Bronnen and that mascot of the

Berlin of Auden and Isherwood, the sympathetic and unfortunate Ernst Toller.

Toller was a born martyr to the *Zeitgeist*. The dates of his biography stand for those of dozens of his contemporaries: born of Jewish parents in Samotschin in 1893; committed suicide in New York 1939. Like so many young Germans of his generation he had welcomed the war enthusiastically. For them, as for Rupert Brooke, the outbreak of hostilities seemed to bring release from the triviality and boredom of everyday existence. For Toller, no doubt, it meant even more. As a Jew lacking firm roots in any 'national' community, he found a new sphere of loyalty in the German fatherland he was summoned to defend. Yet disillusion followed. As for so many members of his generation the war became a trauma, an evil to be fought in himself and in others, a compulsive horror to be lived through again and again without release. For Toller and Brecht and their friends the outward became an inward struggle. For many others, however, for the future Nazis and their hidden allies, the trauma had to be re-lived in the world of reality.

For the Left generally, the First World War was an imperialist war; responsibility for it rested with the *Kaiser* and his generals and their class accomplices abroad. For the extremists, the followers of Liebknecht and the Spartacist movement, the Social Democrats had put themselves in the same boat as the militarists by voting the War Credits in August 1914. The attraction of Spartacus and Bolshevism lay in their apparent innocence; the Revolution alone was pure. The young Toller was flung, a determined rebel, into this turmoil of self-exculpation and polemic. Invalided out of the army in 1916 he joined various left-wing groups in anti-war agitation and ended up at Niederschönhausen in Berlin in a military prison. There he wrote his first play with its very Expressionist title *Die Wandlung. Das Ringen eines Menschen* (literally: 'The Transformation. The Wrestling of a Man').

The play is, of course, blatantly autobiographical. And it is chiefly remarkable in that it describes not only Toller's past—the conversion of a fervent patriot into a pacifist—but also the torments of conscience he was to endure as a leader of the short-lived Bavarian Soviet Republic in April 1919. Like many a would-be Friend of Humanity he had the choice of supporting the extremists in their ruthlessness—they intended to withdraw ration cards from the *bourgeoisie* and to shoot hostages—or of seeing the Socialist experiment fail. He chose the latter, even breaking into a cellar at night to release the threatened hostages, and was for his pains tried for high treason by the triumphant counter-revolution. Yet the pathos of this decision is clearly foreshadowed in *Die Wandlung*. The young hero is told by his sister:

> Many a merit or what seems so today
> You will fling off as one flings off a mask
> Who knows where you will find your proper merit then:
> He who preaches to mankind
> Must first discover mankind in himself.

This is the authentic Expressionist *pathos*. You must believe in humanity before you can change the world, and change the world you must. The people call on Toller's hero to lead their revolution, but he is willing to do so only if each revolutionary will make a declaration of his faith in Man:

SISTER: And where does the road lead?
BROTHER: To Man.
SISTER: And beyond?
BROTHER: Beyond? I care not. I am like a plant rooted
    in the infinite ocean. It is glorious to know that one
    has roots and yet is able to drift.

Toller's hero then speaks to the people in the market-place and one by one they kneel down and cry out: 'We too would be Men!' Whereupon he consents to lead them to the promised land.

To the present-day reader there is something more than a

little ridiculous in this '*O Mensch Pathos*'. But with Toller at least he is gripped and appalled by its genuineness. Undeniably Toller was hysterical and inexperienced; he was only twenty-six when he was made party secretary and Commissar in the Bavarian Red Army. But he did not merely share the outward fate of his generation, its political neuroses, its violence and despair. Where so many refused to admit national defeat or the need of either Right or Left for fundamental inward renewal, he showed willingness to suffer. He gave expression to a faith which, naïve as it was, offered more hope than the acquiescence in the destructive fury of the age Heym and Benn represented.

Echoes of Toller's faith in Man are to be found in the early poems of Auden and Spender, in 'Love, the interest itself in thoughtless heaven' or 'It concerns us all—and human glory'. The experience of meeting Toller and his friends in Berlin clearly left its mark on the budding talents of the English 'thirties—not least on the Expressionist dramas *Ascent of F6* and *Dog beneath the Skin* which Auden and Isherwood were to write together. After Toller's suicide in New York in May 1939 Auden wrote:

> What was it, Ernst, that your shadow unwittingly said?
> O, did the child see something horrid in the woodshed
> Long ago? Or had the Europe which took refuge in your
>   heart
> Already been too injured to get well?

And Auden describes the 'friends who are sad and the enemies who rejoice' being driven away from the grave:

> Lest they should learn without suffering how to forgive.

In the Germany of the Twenties there was no fear of that; few were willing to suffer and none knew how to forgive. And the few who were of Ernst Toller's mind never again had an opportunity to take the lead in politics. We have said that Expressionism cannot be systematized, that it was a cry from the heart. The cry from the heart could be, as with Toller, a

cry of compassion and universal love; it could equally well be
a cry of despair or of fanatical hatred. And as the Twenties proceeded it was the cries of wrath and resentment that became
louder and more insistent. The large-hearted world-bettering
Spartacist sympathizers of 1919 turned into the well-drilled
Stalinist functionaries who were later to return under the aegis
of the Soviets after 1945. And on the Right the disorganized
Berlin Nazis found an all too capable leader in Joseph Goebbels who was dispatched by the *Führer* in 1927 to prepare the
way of the counter-revolution in Red Berlin. The days of the
amateur revolutionaries were over. Art ceased to count except
in the service of the party: Arnolt Bronnen marched with the
Brownshirts, Bertolt Brecht wrote didactic plays in the Agit-
prop manner. The cry was still 'Revolution', but it was
Revolution with the '*O Mensch Pathos*' cut out.

In retrospect the Twenties seem to have been a period of
extraordinary activity, each of its products has an entirely
distinctive flavour, whether Expressionist or not. The year
1919 saw the first great triumph of the German cinema, *The
Cabinet of Dr. Caligari* with Werner Krauss and Conrad Veidt.
The unexpected success of this film with its weird scenery—
'the world seen through the eyes of a madman' it was said—
both at home and abroad, led to more ambitious speculation.
Such films were cheap to produce and their popular Expressionism caught the fancy of a new generation of film-goers.
Indeed many people still derive their conception of the style
from films like *The Student of Prague, Nosferatu—a symphony
of horror, Peter the Great, Siegfried's Death, The Golem,
Pandora's Box.* All these were silent films and produced before
the days of the all-powerful and later Nazified UFA and before the intrusion of Hollywood. After about 1927 the number
of artistically ambitious films decreased sharply. But even after
1927 important films were produced: *The Blue Angel* (1930) with
Marlene Dietrich and Emil Jannings, *Mädchen in Uniform* Pabst's
Kameradschaft, and the film version of the *Threepenny Opera*.

The spate of triumphs in the cinema was not an isolated phenomenon. Most of those who acted in films had already made their reputations on the Berlin stage, and the period between 1900 and 1930 was the Golden Age of theatre in Berlin. In these years 'Theatre'—in the sense of serious experimental theatre—meant Moscow, Berlin, and Paris. Otto Brahm, the Stanislavsky of Berlin, had introduced a technique of Naturalism to present the plays of Ibsen and Hauptmann in the 'nineties. He was soon to be eclipsed after the turn of the century by his brilliant pupil Max Reinhardt, who brought the baroque splendour and psychological sophistication of his native Vienna to the rationalistic north. (One is reminded of Hofmannsthal's sketch of the differences between Prussian and Viennese mentality.) Reinhardt's influence on the technique of the film, particularly his exploitation of light and shadow, was certainly considerable. Yet, strictly speaking, Max Reinhardt belongs to the period 1906–1920. (1906, première of *Ghosts* in his new Kammerspiele; 1906, the splendid panoramic display of his *Oedipus Rex* in the Circus, more like a military tattoo than a tragic drama; 1913, the famous and often repeated production of *A Midsummer Night's Dream*; 1921, *Wozzeck* for the first time in the Deutsches Theater.) After 1920 Reinhardt transferred his attention more and more to Vienna and to the Salzburg Festival which he had founded with Hugo von Hofmannsthal.

In fact Max Reinhardt and his neo-Baroque theatre already belonged to the past. New producers were coming forward, many of them reacting against his methods as he had reacted against the Naturalism of Brahm. Leopold Jessner, already a full-blooded Expressionist, was responsible for sensational productions of the plays of Toller, Kaiser and Hasenclever. A little later the experimental theatre took a political turn with Piscator and his would-be proletarian theatre 'am Nollendorfplatz'. Of all this experimentation Brecht's post-1945 'Theater am Schiffbauerdamm' was the legitimate legatee.

The left-wing element was very much in evidence during the whole period, and indeed increased from year to year. But one should distinguish between the spirit of rebellion of the pre-war generation and the party fanaticism of 1930. Typical of the former was the 'Wandervogel' movement, founded in Berlin in the years before the First World War. It was a more romantic edition of the Boy Scouts, a cross between Baden-Powell and the spirit of young Tieck and Wackenroder. Its attitudes were un-Prussian in the extreme and were part of a much wider revolt against the 'world of the Father' reflected in such Expressionist plays as Hasenclever's *The Son* or Arnolt Bronnen's *Patricide. Wandervogel* was libertarian and individualistic, and more concerned with free love than with free speech. But while the Youth Movement was romantically unpolitical in its beginnings, its post-war successors were to become more and more the protégés and later the instruments of the political parties.

By the early 'twenties the situation resembled that in England ten years later; it was *de rigueur* for intellectuals to be left of centre and to patronize the proletariat. What had been eccentricities with Arno Holz and Gerhart Hauptmann had now become binding orthodoxy. This is not to deny that sympathy often went deeper. The social compassion, for instance, of Alban Berg's *Wozzeck*, first produced at the Staatsoper in 1922, is a profoundly moving and convincing experience. Georg Büchner's play about a poor creature who is bullied by his superiors and murders the wife who has betrayed him with the regimental sergeant-major, was a favourite of the Expressionist left. It is the young Brecht's strongest influence and Toller's *Hinkemann* is little more than a modern version of Büchner's *Wozzeck*: that living disproof of Yeats's assertion that passive suffering is no subject for tragedy.

Not that passive suffering was to the taste of the young people who found their way into *Wandervogel* or Spartacus. They were Nietzscheans to a man in regard to all relics of

Christian slave-morality. Nevertheless the opportunities for protest against the *status quo* were limited; the Prussian police and military machine was (they had been told so often and had cause to know) the most efficient in the world. It was vulnerable only to a practical joker of the calibre of the Captain of Cöpenick. With the outbreak of war any kind of protest could be construed as high treason. On the 1st of May 1916 Liebknecht and Rosa Luxemburg were arrested in Berlin while organizing their first open anti-war demonstration. Only abroad, on neutral soil, could a protest still be made.

In these same weeks while the Battle of the Somme was at its height a group of exiles came together in the Café Voltaire in Zürich (that Zürich where Joyce was writing his *Ulysses* and Lenin, just down the street, was waiting for the sealed train in which the German High Command were to smuggle him into Russia). 'Dada' came into being—a word found by opening a German-French dictionary at random. Dada was designed by its promoters—Hugo Ball, Hans Arp, Tristan Tzara—as a flamboyant protest against the misconduct of the world's affairs. But this time the protest was not directed merely against the *bourgeoisie*: they were comparatively honest. Dada was directed against Art, and against all those whose hypocritical mouthings on the subject of *Kultur* and Western values served to gloss over the brutal and senseless massacres going on outside. The Dadaist could have said with Göring that when he heard the word *Kultur* he reached instinctively for his revolver.

Art exhibitions were held in public lavatories; meetings were arranged at which the audience was deliberately made fun of, poems recited and drowned by a simultaneous clatter of typewriters; and if the evening ended in a brawl—so much the better. Hans Arp and Richard Hülsenbeck later transferred their activities to Berlin where they were joined by George Grosz and the brothers Herzfelde and Heartfield (Hans Herzfelde had changed his name to John Heartfield as a whimsical protest against the general Germanization of place-names at the beginning of the war when the Café Paris became Café Vaterland). Tristan Tzara migrated to Paris where the movement evolved under André Breton's guidance into the more fruitful Surrealism. In both capitals the new doctrine of 'Down with Culture' was fervently preached to the cacophonous accompaniment of saucepan lids and bicycle bells (dubbed 'Bruitisme'). It was a relief from war-time tensions; the Berlin burghers flocked to the meetings and let themselves be shocked and outraged. Dada had its few months of glory. It was soon to be replaced by movements that took the doctrine of 'Down with Culture' a great deal more seriously.

The most gifted member of Dada in Berlin was probably George Grosz. Grosz was a caricaturist of genius and his best period was the decade following the First World War. Political satire in Germany had never worn velvet gloves, but Grosz etched his fat-necked profiteers and smug Berlin *petits bourgeois* in the purest vitriol. It is revealing that he caricatures a class; the toothbrush moustache of the demobbed NCO: the Prussian elementary schoolmaster, all bristles and chokers; the seedy-looking spivs of the Friedrichstrasse, and their friends in high places. But the portraits lose nothing by their anonymity; each could be an Adolf Hitler or an Oswald Spengler. On the features of each there is that flicker of contempt and hatred for the new-born German republic.

During the revolutionary winter of 1918–1919, the Dadaists from Zürich had naturally come into contact with the bickering left-wing groups, and their sympathies were doubtless with the Spartacists of Liebknecht and Rosa Luxemburg. The Social Democrats of Ebert and Noske seemed to have sold out to the middle classes. Ebert had thanked the returning troops from the Reichstag for their heroic services to the Fatherland; he would soon, no doubt, be apeing the *Kultur* hypocrisy of his predecessors. And this—it must have seemed to them—was precisely what did happen. To procure order and civilization Ebert commissioned the *Freikorps* to put down the Spartacist rising in January 1919, during which disturbance Liebknecht and Luxemburg were drowned in the Landwehrkanal. Their last political act had been the foundation of a German Communist party on the model of Lenin's Bolsheviki. And from January 1919 onwards there was no quarter given in the struggle between the gigantic but sluggish SPD (the Socialists) and the minute but fanatical KPD (the Communists).

The left-wing artists and writers were men of the opposition by temperament. But now the SPD was in power. Satirists like George Grosz and Kurt Tucholsky (the true successor to Glassbrenner of the 1848 Revolution) now began to submit the new Weimar Republic to the treatment they had once reserved for the *Kaiser* and his *bourgeois* boot-lickers. Bismarck had said that for the Germans 'le mieux est l'ennemi du bon'; and one reason for the failure of the Weimar experiment was that intellectuals could not reconcile themselves to the idea of a lesser evil. From here began a drift towards the extreme left, at the same time a continuation of the protest against the old order and a search for a new discipline. In a little pamphlet published in 1925 George Grosz and Wieland Herzfelde forswore Dadaism, proclaiming 'the art of the present time is dependent on the *bourgeoisie* and will die with that class' and further 'this Expressionist anarchism must stop!' 'The time is coming', say the repentant Dadaists, 'when the artist will no longer be the Bohemian, sponge-like enemy of society that he was but a healthy clear-thinking worker in the collectivist society.' This is almost the position of Brecht in his Didactic Plays after 1927; only if he is willing to co-operate with the working class in its struggle can the artist hope to redeem his work from insignificance.

Here for the first time Berlin was exposed to the chilly East wind of Marxist-Leninist dogma. But again a distinction should be made between the lively pre-Stalinist Moscow of the Twenties and the grey monotony of the following decades. Mayakovsky and Isaac Babel in literature; Eisenstein and

Pudovkin in the cinema; Wachtangov, Tairoff and Meyer-hold in the Theatre; even Kandinsky and the Constructivists in painting were regarded as the heralds of a new age of revolutionary art. Berlin was Russophile by tradition (thanks to the Holy Alliance and the wars of liberation against Napoleon, when the Cossacks had marched through Berlin in pursuit of the French). The war had been made acceptable to the Social Democrats as a crusade against reactionary Tsarism. Now Berlin had been cut off by the war and still more by the treaty of Versailles from the western capitals, Left and Right began to look hopefully to the East.

Both Russia and Germany were vanquished nations; neither had any reason to love the Western Allies and their swarming protégés in Eastern Europe. The treaty of Rapallo, that shrewd master-stroke of Rathenau, and the military intrigues of General von Seeckt with the Red Army merely carried on a traditional friendship between Moscow and Berlin. To the Left, on the other hand, Moscow had become an inspiring—though not yet infallible—political oracle; the more so, because the new doctrines came wrapped in the same revolutionary *avant-gardisme* then fashionable in Berlin. George Grosz received an invitation to the Kremlin and Lenin declared the young caricaturist to be the hope of proletarian art in Germany. Radek and Bucharin were as much at home in Berlin as in Moscow, writing articles in German for the left-wing press and advising the young revolutionary movement.

In addition Berlin was full of White-Russian refugees. There was a contemporary joke that to cross the Tiergarten from the city centre to Charlottenburg one had to apply for a Russian visa. And the influence of these refugees is discernible in the artistic life of the time—in the theatrical influence at second remove of Stanislavsky and Tairoff on producers like Piscator, and in films like *Peter the Great*, which the Russian producer Buchovetsky made with Emil Jannings. With the beginning of the great slump and the subsequent

rise of Nazism many of these Russian émigrés had to join the
trek of Jewish intellectuals and left-wing politicians towards
the more tolerant societies of the West. This migration began
as early as 1927, the year Trotsky left the Soviet Union. In
that year Kurt Tucholsky chose to live in Switzerland.
In 1930 Mayakovsky committed suicide and Brecht declared in
The Punitive Measure his solidarity with the cause of the
Revolution. The road was open to the burning of the Reichstag, the trials of Dimitroff and of Radek and Bucharin, the
Night of the Long Knives and the whole witches' sabbath of
totalitarianism.

Up till now we have spoken loosely of the Twenties as the
period of political anarchy and artistic vitality between the
years 1910 and 1933. Looked at more closely the essential
Twenties seem to lie between the revolution of November
1918 when the Kings disappeared and the royal censorship
with them, and the stabilization of the currency by Schacht
in 1924. But the period of stabilization—politically the Age of
Stresemann—was a deceptively lucid interval. Too few people
were prepared to forgive and forget, like Stresemann to whom
Briand had cried with superb Gallic pathos before the assembled League of Nations: 'C'est fini, la guerre entre nous.'

The war and the inflation had done their work. The old
ruling classes had been decimated and ruined, the middle
classes were permanently and radically embittered against the
republic. And there were other than economic factors at play:
the decay of the 'Prussian virtues' in general and of sexual
morals in particular. We see this clearly in Christopher Isherwood's *Goodbye to Berlin*. Sally Bowles' prattle echoes that of
her contemporaries: 'I'm supposed to meet a man at the Adlon
at five... and it's six already. Never mind, it'll do the old swine
good to wait. He wants me to be his mistress, but I have told
him I'm damned if I will till he has paid all my debts. Why are
men always such beasts?' This—though Isherwood first came
to Berlin in the late 'twenties—is the legendary Berlin of the

inflation. The years when, as intrigued Anglo-Saxons reported back to their friends at home, it was not unusual for mattresses to be provided for the convenience of guests at the balls of a once so strait-laced Society. No doubt Berlin was every bit as wicked as Mr. Norris and his literary creator could have wished. Yet Isherwood's would-be photographic record of Berlin in the Twenties is not quite the real thing, as he has pointed out himself in retrospective criticism of the books *Mr. Norris Changes Trains* and *Goodbye to Berlin.* For they are fundamentally heartless books written by a clever but rather heartless young man; and Berlin, for all its gay perversion, was in the Twenties a place of suffering.

The story of the fall of the Weimar Republic has often been told. The exiles disputed later among themselves as to who bore the responsibility for its inglorious end. The Communists blamed the Social Democrats and the Social Democrats blamed the Communists for not participating in a popular front against Hitler which neither ever contemplated until Hitler was already master of Germany. Many Anglo-Saxon writers blame Schleicher and the army leaders for their connivance and eventual surrender to the Nazis. Another version has it that von Papen and his industrialist friends were to blame. But Hitler had a number of positive advantages. His party had not been discredited and compromised by the failures of the past. Hitler was something new at a time when millions of Germans felt that things could anyway scarcely be worse than they were. Hitler could afford to offer everybody everything: Socialism to the workers, Nationalism to the *bourgeoisie,* violence to would-be rebels as well as strict authority to those who had wearied of a generation of revolt. The things the Great Magician offered were essentially old and conservative—the *bourgeoisie* knew this well enough—but the presentation was new.

New above all—and this constituted a link between Hitler and the Expressionist visionaries—was the apocalyptic note. '*Das Dritte Reich*' is a concept that can be traced back to

Joachim de Flora in the thirteenth century, a vision of a Third Kingdom of the Holy Ghost which has been cherished by generations of heretics and never quite died out. When the economic crisis broke out in 1929 and the anarchy of the inflation period returned, the German people became more and more susceptible to this apocalyptic extremism. For a time the extreme Left and extreme Right seemed to be running neck and neck. But Communism had a fatal handicap; its revolution had already taken place and the German people had been able to observe it at fairly close range. The German people were sick of the class struggle, sick of unemployment, sick of capitalism, sick of the Jews, sick of democracy, and above all sick of Berlin, that modern Gomorrah and the source of all their ills. There is no very great mystery about Hitler's coming to power. The simplest explanation is the best: the German people chose him.

Chapter 10

THE EAGLE AND THE SWASTIKA

1933–1943

HITLER made no secret of his dislike of Berlin. When he had
to visit the city he brought with him his body-guard of hulking
Bavarian youths, his 'Schutzstaffel' or SS. For the Nazis were
the last disciples of Jean Jacques Rousseau; they believed that
virtue resides in the unspoiled child of nature, in this case in
the hardy peasantry of the Bavarian Alps. Nazism was many
things; a release of adolescent aggression; a self-assertion
of the *petite bourgeoisie*; a movement of discharged NCO's
and provincial gym-instructors; and for many, simply
another ladder to better their social position. Nazism was all
things to all men: a superbly organized blend of Idealism and
Opportunism. There can be no definition of Nazism for it
was both an irrational belief—'The creed is the man, the man is
the movement'—and a chance combination of social forces
which hoped to profit from Adolf Hitler's demagogy—and
were sorely disappointed.

Yet certain strains can be picked out and identified. Two
such strains—and the irony of it is that both were manufactured
originally in Berlin—were Romanticism and Prussianism. The
development of Romanticism has been sketched in these pages.
The introduction of the spiked helmet into the Prussian army

in 1840 was the symbol of its public triumph; Prussian officers
had now to think of themselves as the heirs of Lohengrin and
Parsifal. And we have seen that a reactionary flavour was there
even at the start. Heinrich von Kleist's *Catechism for Germans*
at the time of the Napoleonic wars expounds with horrifying
candour the basic doctrines of Nazism:

> QUESTION: Dost thou love thine Fatherland, my son?
> ANSWER: Yes, father, that I do.
> QUESTION: And why dost thou love it?
> ANSWER: Because it is my Fatherland.
> QUESTION: Dost thou mean because God hath blessed
> it with many fruits and because it is beautified with
> many a work of art and because many heroes, states-
> men and wise men have made its name glorious?
> ANSWER: Not so, my father, thou dost lead me astray.
> QUESTION: I lead thee astray?
> ANSWER: For Rome and Egypt were, as thou hast
> taught me, more richly endowed with works of art
> and all that is great and glorious than is Germany.
> Nevertheless, if fate would have it that thy son
> should live in these countries, he would be filled
> with sadness and never be so glad as he is now in
> Germany.
> QUESTION: Why dost thou love Germany?
> ANSWER: My father, I have already told thee!
> QUESTION: Thou hast told me?
> ANSWER: Because it is my Fatherland.

The irrational fanaticism of this is reminiscent at once of
the Rhinelander Dr. Joseph Goebbels, the man whom the
Führer had singled out to deal with the argumentative Berliners; with both Kleist and Goebbels it is Romantic Nihilism
expounded by a skilled dialectician. Goebbels was a Jesuit-
schooled Rhinelander, a very different kettle of fish from the
beer-swilling, Jew-baiting storm-troopers who appreciated
this much of the new Romanticism: that it implied a glorifi-
cation of themselves. The older Romanticism had invested the
Emperor and the princes with the tinsel of Gothic Revivalism.

The new cult with the Bavarian Heinrich Himmler as its high priest turned to a mystical adoration of '*das Volk*'.

Prussianism was another matter. The Prussians had not been prone to Mysticism nor, until the mid-nineteenth century, to Romanticism. At its best Prussianism had represented something to be respected: Kantian ethics and selfless devotion to duty. Only later, as it became stereotyped and mass-produced under Bismarck and Moltke, did it suggest the Philistine Jingoism of a Victorian public school. Yet even at this period it could still produce a man like Moltke himself, a man of fundamental modesty despite his famed *hauteur*. The Prussians believed in a *Bescheidenheit der Leistung*—'a modesty of achievement'; and the true criticism of the Prussian is not that he lacked modesty but that he lacked humility. He lacked humility because he had taken the state for his God and was too confident of the ultimate value of his achievement. With the Nazis, however, the old ideals of *mehr sein als scheinen* fell into decay and a naked worship of the state emerged. The Nazi sought religious satisfaction directly or vicariously in the pursuit of power.

Prussia certainly contributed other elements to the witches' brew. After the First World War Oswald Spengler issued a short pamphlet with the title *Prussianism and Socialism*, arguing that the ideals and methods of the Socialists were essentially those long preached and practised in the colonial territories of North-Eastern Germany. He suggested that as Socialism had grown out of Prussianism now both should merge, on Hegelian lines, to form a new and greater whole, a 'nationally-minded' Socialism. The pamphlet is a model of specious and fantastic argument; the virtues of the English and the Prussians respectively are traced to their descent from the Vikings and the Teutonic Knights. These two extremes, 'rugged individualism' and 'State Socialism', are, Spengler argues, bound to misunderstand one another and their wars be like the Punic wars that can end only with the razing of

Carthage to the ground. Berlin was a hive of reactionary quacks in the late 'twenties and early 'thirties; writers like Ernst Jünger and Möller van den Bruck and Ernst von Salomon (who had taken part in the assassination of Walter Rathenau) made their voices heard above the left-wing chorus with demands for a 'Conservative Revolution'.

But the Prussian ideals in their original form were dead. The true bearers of these values, the *Junker* aristocrats, the army, and the higher civil service had withdrawn from the immediate political arena. They knew—and here they were not wrong—that Germany could not be ruled again as it had been before 1918; the Revolution had been a vote of no confidence in the old Prussian system. Their ambition now was to hold on to their vast estates east of the Elbe and secure commissions in the much-reduced army for their younger sons. Bismarck's Prussian ruling class had become merely one pressure group among many others, unable to reconcile itself either to Social Democracy or to the Catholic centre or to the new right-wing Radicalism. In the event, they played a nearly passive role in the transfer of power to the Nazis. It was the astute Hitler who duped and exploited the army leaders and the industrialists, not vice versa.

Prussianism had somehow to be *'gleichgeschaltet'* into the Third Reich, being far too valuable to be left outside and still too powerful to be liquidated. And the *'Gleichschaltung'* of Prussian legend and tradition was the occasion of Goebbels' most brilliant theatrical coup. On the 21st of March 1933 units of the SS and of a former guards regiment formed a common guard of honour for Hitler and Hindenburg at the grave of Frederick the Great. In the presence of the leaders of the army and the other representatives of the state, the aged Hindenburg solemnly took Adolf Hitler's hands in his while the bells of the Garnisonskirche in Potsdam rang out *'Üb immer Treu und Redlichkeit'* ('Loyal and honest shalt thou be'). It is not certain whether the aged president really knew what he was doing. He had sold his Prussian birthright for a very sorry mess of pottage. It was left to the men of the 20th of July 1944 to save what they could of Prussian honour.

It is as well to be frank about Nazi Germany in the 'thirties. For the average citizen these were happy years. Unemployment vanished, the currency became stable, there was greater social security and a new sense of national pride and prosperity. Above all, the chronic violence of the Weimar period seemed at last to have been overcome (actually it had only disappeared from sight—into Dachau and Buchenwald). Likewise the notorious immorality; no longer did male prostitutes display their charms openly on the Tauentzienstrasse and the Kurfürstendamm. Hitler was determined to make the city a worthy capital of the future Greater German Reich. He disliked the city but he had no choice. With her four and a quarter million inhabitants she was the largest city in Germany and, after London, the largest in Europe. The road leading westward from the Brandenburger Tor to Charlottenburg and beyond had already been extended under the *Kaiser* to form Berlin's only radial outlet to the March of Brandenburg. Hitler had it widened and beautified and called it the East-West Axis. The Siegessäule from the Franco-Prussian War was removed from in front of the Reichstag and re-erected on the new Axis.

Building continued during the 'twenties and 'thirties in most suburbs of Berlin, though since 1921 these had been merged into a Greater Berlin with roughly the frontiers of post-1945 four-sector Berlin. In Dahlem the Kaiser Wilhelm Scientific Institutes where Max Planck, Einstein and Otto Hahn had worked were systematically enlarged. Around them the tycoons of the Third *Reich* built their imposing villas in the gay old Teutonic style: pine-wood rafters and horses' heads became the rage. A rather different style was obligatory for public institutions; cliffs of sheer ferro-concrete enlivened by sculptures of happy peasant life. But, to be fair, the Socialist component of the new creed was not entirely neglected. There

were new blocks of workers' flats in Wittenau and Neukölln.
Yet the rate of building was not comparable to the first *Gründer-*
jahre after 1870 or the second which set in after 1900. The
greater part of Berlin had been built by 1914 and the style had
not changed for the better. Only in the 'twenties for a brief
moment did Gropius, Mies van der Rohe, and Erich Mendelssohn have an opportunity to build in the city. And Hans
Poelzig's Radio Station and Exhibition Halls and the Shell
House also deserve a mention.

But the man in the street got a reassuring impression of
directed energy and reconstruction in public life, and it would
be foolish to deny that he preferred it to the anarchy of the
Weimar period. Two products of the Third *Reich* impressed
him particularly: the vast new airfield at Tempelhof and the
Olympia Stadium. Both tended towards the grandiose and yet
preserved a certain massive simplicity reminiscent of the designs of Schinkel's friend and teacher Friedrich Gilly. And the
Berliners were not alone in praising the monster outlay for the
Olympic games in 1936. Anglo-Saxons came home full of
enthusiasm for the bold planning of the new dictatorship and
its appreciation of the values of sportsmanship. Berlin was a
revelation: the shops so clean! The people so honest! The
streets so full of purposeful activity! It was the Nazis' greatest
triumph; all the world had come to honour the new Germany,
and not a drop of foreign blood had yet been shed. For the
Berliners, if they are frank, these were among the best years of
their lives.

And it is necessary to emphasize this; for many Berliners
have made a private act of oblivion in regard to the Third *Reich*.
It is impossible for those who lived through it to see it except
as a whole: the apocalyptic hopes of 1933, the comparatively
quiet and prosperous years leading up to Munich; the sudden
and unexpected victories of 1939–1941 and the equally sudden
and unexpected defeats that led to the collapse of 1945. And it
is inevitably of the collapse and the subsequent misery that

people think when the question is put: 'Whether perhaps Adolf wasn't right after all. . . .'

Bertolt Brecht wrote in his Danish exile *Fear and Misery of the Third Reich*, an attempt to portray the 'real' Nazi Germany. This play shows more clearly than any other how political dogma can warp even the keenest observation of life. In almost every scene we hear of concentration camps, shootings, Jew-baiting, starving proletarians and well-fed *bourgeois*, political violence and corruption, and the more or less cynical accommodation of the citizen to this state of affairs. No one could deny that these things happened, and Brecht's analysis of the impact of politics on the individual is masterly. And yet it is a misleading picture; it is the typical portrait of his home country by a political exile. No doubt for the artists and intellectuals of the Twenties, for Brecht himself, for Thomas Mann, Arthur Koestler, George Grosz, Albert Einstein it rang true as a record of these terrible years. And yet if one was not a Jew or a Socialist or otherwise down on the Nazi black list why should one quarrel with a political *fait accompli*?

So the Berliners joined in the music with the rest, cheered the endless processions along Unter den Linden and flocked to Goebbels' rabble-rousing speeches in the Sportpalast. But many of them went merely out of curiosity; and others retired to cultivate their allotments. Private life was not at first radically affected. The man in the street made his little adjustments and compromises with the life around him. There was still good theatre: Heinrich George, Emil Jannings and Gustaf Gründgens were among the many who did not or could not leave Germany. And there was still Furtwängler with the Philharmonic. The Jews were being gradually squeezed out of the national life. Some tried to help them; the rest passed by on the other side. Like Brecht's Galileo they murmured: 'Unhappy the land that has need of heroes!'

But the *Führer* did need heroes: as many of them as he could lay his hands on. The Saar, Austria, the Sudetenland were

swallowed up by the *Reich*; mothers-of-four received medals
for services rendered to the Fatherland. The patriotic clap-
trap that had flourished during the First World War now re-
emerged cruder and more strident. It was as though Kurt
Tucholsky and George Grosz had never been. For the older
generation, the Prussian headmasters and senior civil servants,
Nazism, though a distastefully plebeian phenomenon, seemed
at least to mark a return to traditional values. They agreed
with Hindenburg that 'the Bohemian corporal' was a temporary necessity; he could be dispensed with later when the
time was ripe for a restoration of the monarchy. '*Gleichschaltung*' was a process which had left their positions unscathed.

Hardest hit—indeed hit so hard that the possibility of
resistance was eliminated from the start—were the workers'
organizations. By throwing their leaders into concentration
camps and confiscating all party property the Nazis soon broke
the model organizations of the SPD and the KPD. The lack
of any effective left-wing resistance movement is easily explained; brutality proved a successful short-term policy. The
number of 'Weimar republicans', on the other hand, who were
prepared to become fellow-travellers of the Nazis was not very
great. The parties of the right and centre went into voluntary
dissolution; their members went back to their board rooms and
professorial studies and country estates. Among the intellectuals there was one eminent renegade, the Expressionist
Gottfried Benn; but after lending himself to a couple of ill-
considered radio eulogies of the new regime and being publicly
ex-communicated by the Mann family connection, he too beat a
rapid retreat into private life. Later, in 1938, after his writings
had been banned as 'degenerate' he re-entered the army as a
medical officer, coining a much-quoted *bon mot* to the effect
that 'the army has become the only respectable form of emigration'.

The position of the army was anomalous in the Nazi system.
Every other aspect of public life had been '*gleichgeschaltet*';

whether Nazified like the Youth Movement or liquidated like the trade unions. But the army remained: Hitler could not afford to challenge the power of this Prussian enclave in his otherwise obedient empire. In previous Berlin revolutions the army had played an active, if reactionary part: General Wrangel had put down the revolution of 1848 and the *Freikorps* had disposed of the Spartacists in January 1919. In January 1933, however, the army made no move. A year later when their own General Schleicher was murdered in his Grunewald villa by Nazi gangsters, they again made no move. When Hindenburg died that summer they took their oath of loyalty to Adolf Hitler as head of state without a murmur.

By 1938, however, the gentlemen of the General Staff in the Bendlerstrasse were thoroughly alarmed at the *Führer*'s policies. General Beck, the real successor of Moltke, tried in vain to persuade his colleagues to move against Hitler, and himself resigned in protest against a war policy that he feared would be the ruin of Germany. It was during the Munich crisis that feelers first began to go out from the anti-Nazi army leaders to other known anti-Nazi elements in Berlin. Former politicians, the Conservative Goerdeler, the Catholic Jakob Kaiser, and the Social Democrat Julius Leber began to meet secretly in the villas of mutual friends in Dahlem and Wannsee.

The Munich crisis blew over and the popularity of Hitler knew no bounds. But the leaders of a potential Resistance movement now existed, and during the following years the net of contacts was widened to include industrialists like Robert Bosch from Stuttgart, churchmen like the young theologian Dietrich Bonhoeffer and independents like Helmut von Moltke, the great-nephew of Bismarck's Moltke, and his friend Count Yorck. For a time Pastor Niemöller and his friends at the village church in Dahlem formed a centre of resistance, but in 1938 he too was removed to a concentration camp. The opposition groups looked more and more to the army as the one independent force able to rid Germany of Hitler. The

Prussian army, from being the guarantor of the *status quo* under the Hohenzollerns, had become to its own surprise and discomfort a potentially subversive element in the state.

Ulrich von Hassell's diary gives a picture of the fluctuating moods in conservative circles at this period. Himself shelved by Ribbentrop after a period as German Ambassador in Rome, his diaries reflect perfectly both the personal resentment and the patriotic anguish of the old ruling class. Von Hassell would wander disconsolately round Berlin: breakfast at the Adlon with Schacht; lunch at his club with General von Witzleben; semi-conspiratorial gatherings at Beck's or von Moltke's in the evening. Every night the same theme would be mooted: Hitler must go, decent people must stand together, the army must make a move, the other side must be approached. It is impossible to doubt the sincerity of von Hassell and the deep shame he and his friends felt at their government's action—yet what was to be done? Hitler's popularity after Munich vitiated any attempt to remove him from power.

At the outbreak of war von Hassell wrote: 'For the first time I have noted a sort of *Götterdämmerung* mood among the Nazis.' But once again the Nazis were carried forward on the flood of military success in the Polish campaign. Von Hassell and his friends persisted. Contact was made with the Allied Powers through Otto John, and through Dietrich Bonhoeffer who met the Bishop of Chichester secretly on a visit to Sweden. But the long-awaited ebb in Hitler's fortunes never came; right into the terrible Russian winters of 1941–42 his luck seemed to hold. And while his luck held it was clear that the German people would follow him as the French people had once followed Napoleon. The Berliners hurrahed as shamelessly as anyone in the *Reich*: did not the victory over France seem to close the account finally for the humiliations of Versailles? It was only the older generation, men like von Hassell who had fought in the trenches in 1914 and who knew something of the outside world, who remained unconvinced by the

Great Magician. And these men Goebbels had long ago written off as defeatists.

Joseph Goebbels was by far the most important figure in Berlin throughout the Nazi era. It was he who had won Berlin for Nazism. He described the battle for control of the press and his nightly excursions protected by SA thugs into reddest Berlin, Wedding and Neukölln, in his *Kampf um Berlin*. It was he who had organized the farcical ceremony in the Garnisonskirche in Potsdam, and, of the bread and circuses of the Third *Reich*, it was he who was responsible for the latter. Goebbels was the right man for Berlin: the Berliner liked talking, but Goebbels talked faster; the Berliner was quick-witted, but Goebbels had a mind trained in the subtle and ancient school of the Jesuits. The other Nazis were simple-minded ruffians; Hitler himself was crafty rather than intelligent. But Dr. Goebbels was an ex-intellectual, a renegade from civilization, a pupil of the famous Jewish Professor of German literature at Heidelberg, Friedrich Gundolf.

As long as all went well with the *Führer*'s policies Goebbels had an easy task. It was only when the curve of success began to sink that his abilities really came into their own and his intellectual Nihilism emerged. In January 1943 Field Marshal Paulus surrendered at Stalingrad after months of bitter fighting. The *Wehrmacht* had lost 250,000 men. Almost simultaneously the Anglo-American air-raids on Berlin were stepped up in intensity. Göring had boasted once from his palatial new Air Ministry in the Wilhelmstrasse that if a single Allied plane reached Berlin he would eat his hat. But Göring was now sulking in the Bavarian Alps; he neither ate his hat nor could he conjure any more fighters or AA guns out of it.

For Goebbels, on the other hand, Stalingrad was a gift of fate: with this instrument he would drive the German people into the abyss. At a great rally in the Sportpalast he yelled at the hysterical masses the challenge: 'Do you want Total War?' And the masses yelled back a terrible hypnotized 'Ja'. Every defeat, every privation now became a whip with which Goebbels could lash the German people to yet greater effort and greater sacrifice. The Casablanca Declaration set the seal on his propaganda for Total Warfare; the door was bolted, the German people must fight to the bitter end. Wagner had long been the Nazis' favourite composer, now Siegfried's funeral march and Brunhilde's ride into the flames resounded from the studios of Berlin Radio night after night. Goebbels was celebrating the orgies of Nihilism; for the German people it was to be total victory or total oblivion, *das Nichts.*

Chapter 11

THE TWILIGHT OF THE GODS

1943-1945

HOW was it that the Nazis had kept their grip on Germany and above all on Berlin, the city where no reactionary had dared show his face in the early Twenties? What had happened to the earnest discontented intellectuals in their shabby cafés around whom a Continental revolution is supposed to crystallize? Why in a city of 4,000,000 people could not the masses resist, at least passively, the new tyranny of the Swastika and the Eagle? One answer is that of orthodox Leninism: the workers can do nothing without their 'General Staff', a disciplined revolutionary élite. And the trained cadres of the SPD and KPD had been physically removed from the scene. After Dimitroff's public mockery of Göring at the Reichstag arson trial, protest from within the *Reich* ceased to be practicable. The Socialist party intellectuals and as many of the rank and file as were able fled to Prague, Paris, and London. The Communists made their way by stages to Moscow. Such of them as survived the great purges returned in 1945 in the baggage of the Red Army and helped the Russians to impose the Socialism-from-above of the German Democratic Republic. Others like Ernst Thälmann, the Communist party leader, vanished into the concentration camps in 1933 and never again emerged.

The number of those physically in a position to resist

Nazism was always extremely limited, if by resistance is meant more than the shrug of the shoulder, the mental reservation and the joke about Goebbels' club foot or Göring's appetite. And there was another factor. The number of people who really knew what was happening was very small. Only those in high government positions or on active service knew much about the extent of either the Jewish massacres or the military weakness of the *Wehrmacht*. It was among such men, few of them intellectuals, most of them conservative by upbringing, who were in a position both to know and to act, that the bomb plot of the 20th of July 1944 began to take shape.

In the autumn of 1943 a young colonel, badly wounded in Africa and now seconded to the General Staff in the Bendlerstrasse, began to frequent the meetings of the would-be conspirators. It was the autumn of the first thousand bomber raids on Berlin; driving to work in the morning it was common to find whole new sections of the city reduced to rubble and ash and twisted girder. One night the famous antique-shop quarter near the Tiergarten had disappeared; another the old shopping and amusement centre of the Leipzigerstrasse and the Kurfürstendamm. The apocalyptic vision of Georg Heym's *Der Krieg* had become horrific actuality. But as the need to put an end to the destruction and slaughter became more urgent, the position of the conspirators grew more desperate. In 1943 Bonhoeffer and several others had been arrested by the Gestapo. Unconditional surrender seemed wilfully to rule out a compromise peace with any non-Nazi German government and thus make the efforts of Goerdeler and Beck seem doubly futile. There remained the one argument, the deeply Prussian and idealist argument, that 'the thing must be done, because it must be done'; as a symbolic act to save the nation's honour even though the chances of political success had become very small.

This categorical imperative was essentially Count Stauffenberg's argument. He knew, as did all responsible people by the autumn of 1943, that Germany had lost the war. He also knew that Hitler would destroy Germany rather than surrender. Therefore Hitler must be killed. Stauffenberg had all the ruth-lessness of the idealist as man of action. He had been one of the initiates of the esoteric circle of the poet Stefan George and he possessed a demonic energy in his now mutilated body (he had lost an eye and a hand during Rommel's retreat in Tunisia). It was Stauffenberg who rallied the faint-hearted generals and gingered up the politicians to the point of action. On the 20th of July he himself flew to East Prussia with the bomb in his brief-case and deposited it under the table at Hitler's morning staff conference.

It is a matter of history that the brief-case was shifted to the outside of one of the heavy wooden legs of the table and that Hitler suffered no more than shock and punctured ear-drums. It is not so well known that the *putsch* could have succeeded in Berlin if it had not been for Goebbels' acuteness and the mis-management of the conspirators. During the late afternoon a company under the command of Major Remer had been detailed by General Beck and his friends at *Wehrmacht* Headquarters in the Bendlerstrasse to surround the government buildings in the Wilhelmstrasse and on Unter den Linden. Remer did as he was told. But he had neither been initiated into the plot nor did he know clearly what and whose orders he was supposed to be obeying. When he attempted to arrest the *Reichspropa-gandaminister* in his office, Goebbels had the wit to receive him calmly and politely and ask him to take a seat. Remer explained pedantically that he had orders from the Bendlerstrasse to arrest a number of leading Nazis in Berlin. Goebbels did not need to be told twice. He rang through to East Prussia, de-manded to speak to the *Führer* personally, and handed the receiver to Major Remer. At the familiar deep growl Remer drew himself up: '*Jawohl, mein Führer*'. He was promoted Colonel on the spot and told to march to the Bendlerstrasse and arrest Beck, Stauffenberg and their friends. Once again, Remer did as he was told.

By the late evening the conspiracy had failed. Beck asked leave to commit suicide, Stauffenberg and three others were summarily shot in the courtyard of the Bendlerstrasse (renamed Stauffenbergstrasse after the war). Within a few weeks the Gestapo had extracted in the cellars of the near-by Albrechtstrasse all the information they needed. Freisler, apeing Vyshinsky in Moscow five years before, started his examinations before the People's Court. For the first time in Prussian history a field-marshal, the aged von Witzleben, was convicted of high treason. The accused were systematically insulted; Freisler spat in their faces. Von Witzleben had had his braces taken away and was compelled pathetically to hoist his trousers throughout the proceedings. Alone among the conspirators Count Yorck, a descendant of the General Yorck of the Napoleonic wars, managed to blurt out a defence of his actions. Then he and the others were hurried back to Plötzensee prison where they were slowly strangled to death—a film of the executions being made for the private satisfaction of the *Führer*. During the summer and autumn of 1944 thousands of suspects were arrested by the Gestapo; 5,000 army officers alone were implicated in the plot and executed. Of those not summarily dispatched the majority were dragged from one concentration camp and prison to another, finally like Admiral Canaris and Dietrich Bonhoeffer to be killed by SS squads on the eve of liberation by the Allies. Only a very few like General Speidel or Moltke's friend Gerstenmaier (today president of the Federal Parliament) managed to survive the holocaust.

These men, it has been said, fell victim to the Nemesis of Power; what took place in the cellars of the Albrechtstrasse and in Plötzensee in the Berlin winter of 1944–1945 was the last act in a tragic history. Prussia had always in the past had men ready to sacrifice their lives, but the cause for which they had made their sacrifice had been Prussia herself. They professed that pagan religion of the State which Chesterton condemned when he called Prussia 'a patch of eighteenth-century heresy'. In every generation the great *Junker* families Fontane describes in his *Rambles in the March of Brandenburg* were bled white on the battlefields. The figures for the casualties in the two World Wars are eloquent.

The following famous *Junker* families lost:

	von Bülow	von Arnim	von Kleist	von Wedel	von der Schulenburg
First World War	33	24	—	22	10
Second World War	35	33	17	29	14

But these had the good fortune to be killed in action. No accurate record is available of those liquidated by the Gestapo or shot out of hand by the Russians in 1945. Nor of those—chiefly women and children—who froze or starved to death during the great trek to the West. Whatever guilt they may have borne for the hubris of former generations and for their connivance in Hitler's schemes of world conquest—and they bear less than some others—it was certainly on Prussia that the sword of the avenger fell.

Yet one cannot speak of the Nemesis of Power alone. It was not only worship of power that had sustained them. Prussia had been also the country of Kantian philosophy and Pietist religion. And the witness of the letters from Berlin prisons that survive from that terrible winter is a decidedly Christian witness. The Prussian names are there: Elisabeth von Thadden, Ernst von Harnack (son of the theologian), Ewald von Kleist, leader of the religious-minded Conservatives in Prussia, Count Yorck, Erwin Planck (son of the physicist) and two men who are properly to be numbered among the Protestant Martyrs: Dietrich Bonhoeffer and Helmut von Moltke. It was the Nazi wish that if they failed at least there should be no élite left in Germany to lead her back to decency and civilization. Nazi thoroughness in this respect left a terrible gap for post-war Germany to fill.

The last generation of Prussians left Germany a legacy of a

L

different sort in the letters of Bonhoeffer and Moltke. The former's letters from his prison in Berlin-Tegel contain some of the profoundest revaluations of Christianity in our time. (Writing in the shadow of death he passionately preached a 'this-worldly' Christianity.) Moltke, in his last letters to his wife from prison at Plötzensee, writes of his aversion to the role of martyr with the nonchalance of an aristocrat during Robespierre's terror, but adds with quiet pride that he was skilful enough in cross-examination to force Freisler to a not insignificant confession. He was being condemned, Moltke wished to insist, not for any specific thing. He had been passionately opposed on religious grounds to the assassination of Hitler. He was being condemned neither as a landowner nor as a Prussian nor as a German. It was his humble pride to have been condemned merely as a Christian and to have provoked Freisler's outburst: 'Count Moltke, you Christians and we National Socialists have one thing in common, and only one, we demand the loyalty of the whole man.' It was only a pity, Moltke wrote, that the ambiguity of this utterance should have been lost on Freisler.

Helmut von Moltke was executed in Plötzensee on the 23rd of January 1945. A few weeks later Freisler himself was killed in an air-raid. But by then a very different mood had taken hold of the city. In the early summer of 1944 it had been obvious only to those with other sources of information than the Goebbels-controlled press and radio that Germany would be defeated. After the invasion of Normandy had succeeded only the few fanatical Nazis among the German generals still believed in final victory; even Rommel, once Hitler's blue-eyed boy, now offered his services to the conspirators.

Had Stauffenberg's bomb killed Hitler there is little doubt that the army and the civil service would have rallied behind Beck and Goerdeler and that the new government would have sued for an armistice in the West. Whether they would have obtained one is another question. From what is now known it is clear that Roosevelt at least would have kept faith with the Russians and have insisted on his formula of unconditional surrender: on this point the conspirators were unduly optimistic. But it is true that if the war had been stopped in July 1944, many millions of human lives could have been saved, almost as many people being killed after this date as were killed in the first five years of the war.

And by February 1945 even those who had refrained from listening in to the BBC knew that the war was lost. The Berliners have always been a sceptical race, and the ruins of their city were a palpable antidote to the hysterical secret-weapon propaganda. The magic of the Third *Reich* evaporated so quickly that, in the autumn of 1944, it was necessary to cheer the faint-hearted with an order that all party-members must wear their badges in public. But as the first refugees poured in from the East, the mood changed from shoulder-shrugging indifference to the fate of the Nazi regime to a numb awareness of the approaching Red Army.

At the beginning of the winter Hitler had left his 'Wolf's Lair' in East Prussia and returned to direct the war from the *Führerbunker* in Berlin, an iceberg of ferro-concrete submerged in the garden of the Chancellery. Since 1941 the war had been for Hitler the campaign in the East; losses in Africa or in the West ceased to count. The sea bored him and he refused to read accounts of the destruction from the air. It was the struggle against Russia that filled his mind. Stalingrad had been a mighty Battle of the Titans. The future of the world—such was the run of bed-time conversation in the *Führerbunker*—would go to the masters of the 'Eurasian Heartland'; Stalin was 'a barbarian, of course, but the hell of a chap'.

By the late winter of 1944 the Russians had reached the Oder, fifty miles from Berlin. Enough refugees had passed through Berlin on their way to the West (and the hope of capture by the Americans) to confirm the worst of Goebbels' anti-Russian propaganda. There was no choice for the *Volkssturm*—the

Home Guard—of boys and old men and the shattered divisions
of the Eastern front but to participate in a second Battle of the
Titans upon which the *Führer* was brooding in his concrete
cavern. At length the *Führer* revealed his will to his assembled
paladins; he would not make his last stand in the Bavarian
Alps as Nazi mythology had assumed. The *Führer* would
render the unworthy capital city of his Third *Reich* the honour
of becoming the German Stalingrad.

But it was not yet 'five minutes past twelve'. Despite the
air-raids and the flood of wretched half-frozen refugees from
East Prussia, Pomerania and Silesia, the city still kept up
appearances during that winter. When the bombing began the
majority of those who had relations in the country had been
evacuated; by the end of the war perhaps a million Berliners
had found refuge in Bavaria or the West. Yet something of
Berlin's fame as a centre of wild, not to say wicked, night-life
still lingered on in the dives off the Friedrichstrasse and the
Kurfürstendamm. The ministries had found themselves
country houses in the March or carried on below ground level
in less splendid versions of the *Führerbunker*.

Berlin during this last winter was still recognizably Prussian.
Junkers in grey, blue and, alas, even black officers' uniforms
still met in the bars of the Adlon or the Kaiserhof; their conversation, once restricted to pig-sticking and the price of corn,
now took a more serious turn. Young Moltke, it was murmured, had always been a queer sort of fellow; half-Red, half-
Christian Scientist. 'His father had broken down as chief of
staff in 1914, shown none of the spirit of the Old Man at
Sadowa in 1866. . . . Case of degeneracy, by gad! There are
still decent chaps at the top though! Fellows like von Rund-
stedt and von Weizsäcker would keep us on the rails. Hitler?
Well, the *Führer*'s a genius in his way, of course, and genius
is an unaccountable thing: he's done it before and he'll do it
again. Himmler? Affable chap . . . bad business that with the
Jews of course, but they'd asked for it, the swine. Remember

that fellow Rathenau for instance! Goebbels? A nasty piece of work, if you like, a little runt of an intellectual, but gifted—no doubt of it. . . . Just the stuff for the masses. . . . Indispensable for national morale.' And so on and so on. Normalcy kept her face. The sirens wailed and the radio exhorted to yet greater efforts. The heirs of Fehrbellin and Waterloo and Sadowa sipped gloomily at their cocktails.

Berlin has always been a city of moods, though the individual Berliner likes to think of himself as a model of hard-headed *Vernunft*. The Berliner has as much *Gemüt* as the next man, but it lies deeper and is prickly to the touch. There is much of the American in the Berliner; you have only to scratch the toughness to reveal the sentimentality. Like an American he thinks of himself as a rugged individualist; the Berliners too are the children of pioneers and have the pioneer virtues of toughness and adaptability. Yet to outside observers the individualism of which Americans and Berliners are so proud often seems a very superficial thing. In reality they all think alike, though they'd slog you one if you told them so. The Berliner cultivated his cheek no doubt to defend himself against the bad old Prussia of police snoopers and press censorship, but the gesture has become habitual: *il faut se défendre —man muss sich wehren.*

The Berliners should be the last people to swallow any *Weltanschauung* whole; especially when preached by those in authority and blared at them day by day in cinema and factory canteen. The best jokes at the expense of the Nazis were made in Berlin and they reverberated thence from one end of the *Reich* to the other. Berlin certainly profited from its immense size. In the German small town Big Brother could keep a check on the opinions of his fellow-citzens: in Berlin this was impossible. Many Jews were hidden, often for years, from the eyes of the SS. Berlin could never be *gleichgeschaltet* as thoroughly as the Nazis would have liked. Nevertheless, even the Berliners' *Gemüt* did not lie so deep that it could not be manipulated by

Dr. Goebbels and his staff. No one believed those stories of Russian soldiers raping defenceless German women. Berlin had always been stoutly Russophile. Resentment was felt much more at the 'cowardly Tommies' who were systematically wrecking the city from the air. Yet for most people resistance to the Nazis seemed a hopeless prospect. Germany was to be dismembered; even, one heard on the radio, to be reduced to a second-rate agrarian power (the Morgenthau plan had been a gift to Goebbels). It was better to do one's duty as father and grandfather had done—good Prussian soldiers all in their blue uniforms among the bric-à-brac on the parlour mantelpiece. And soon grandfather and great-grandson found themselves serving together in the hastily improvised *Volkssturm* of March 1945.

Like Stendhal's hero on the battlefield of Waterloo the *Volkssturm* recruit had little sense of governing purpose and direction in the ensuing struggle. The one young writer who might have become the Stendhal of the battle of Berlin, Felix Hartlaub, was himself one of the thousands of anonymous victims of Hitler's *Götterdämmerung*. But what we possess of Hartlaub's writings, his brilliant pieces of reportage on life in the *Wehrmacht* headquarters, suggest that the ironic individual eye would have been a finer recording instrument in the fury of such a battle than the epic pieces of, say, Theodor Plivier's *Berlin*.

For the totalitarian state at war is a sprawling monster. If in the first months of the Russian campaign the Nazi system did not belie its slogan '*Deutschtum ist Organisation*', by 1944 the Nazi armies were in continuous and disorderly retreat. It was not merely that the *Wehrmacht* was fantastically outnumbered, the Russians attacking with a superiority of ten to one; there was a historical complex at work. The Nazis, true heirs of the Romantics, had taught the German people to think historically; every decision of the *Führer* was a 'world-historical decision'. Hitler had attacked Russia on the same day of the year as Napoleon and was soon inclined to think of his French predecessor as but another 'dwarf' in the company of Franz Josef and William II. But it was an unfortunate comparison. Every German schoolboy, however hastily he had been thrown into uniform, knew what had been the fate of Napoleon in Russia, and some may have known that he chose the better part of valour on the return journey. It may or may not be to Hitler's credit that he did not do this. But then Hitler's temperament was different: irrational, demonic, with more than a dash of the Teutonic death wish. With some primitive layer of his mind Hitler had the gift of reading the submerged wishes and fears of his people and of giving utterance to the inarticulate. And until the winter disasters in Russia it was a reciprocal relationship. Thereafter the masses still kept their faith in the *Führer*, indeed kept it to the bitter end with a pathetic belief in the Great Magician's powers.

Hitler on the other hand began to lose contact with the world of reality. Like many a German Romantic he drifted from ecstatic vision into the twilight of lunacy. At the end Hitler lived alone in the company of his myths. There was the myth of the two Titans, Stalin and himself, deciding the future of the world between them amid the ruins of Stalingrad and Berlin. The Western front interested him temporarily again during the Ardennes campaign of December 1944. Otherwise he had only contempt for his Anglo-Saxon opponents. But then Hitler was an Austrian. To an Austrian the enemy is in the East whether he be Turk or Slav. The Prussians had always been eager for Russian friendship. And Prussian history, too, contributed its share with the myth of Frederick the Great. Goebbels used to read aloud from Carlyle's *History of Frederick the Great*, the *Führer*'s favourite book, during the last days. Particularly welcome was the passage where Carlyle describes the so-called 'miracle of the house of Brandenburg', when Frederick in an apparently hopeless position is saved by the death of the old Tsar and the accession of his devoted admirer

Catherine. Then hope had come from the East: was there perhaps still the chance of a deal with the latest master of the Kremlin?

On the 11th of April Roosevelt died: the miracle seemed to have occurred. But Goebbels' predictions of a conflict between Russia and the Western powers were premature. The Americans swept across Central Germany and sealed off the escape route to the south. Göring left Berlin; Goebbels resolved to stay and share the fate of his *Führer*. On the 20th of April, Hitler's birthday, the Red Army began its assault on the city. 'Stalin's pipe organs' proceeded to finish off what the thousand-bomber raids had failed to demolish. Hitler issued his Stalingrad order to defend the city to the last and made it known that there would be no repetition of Paulus' treachery. But this time the rhetoric did not work. The only incentive to fight on was the knowledge that SS squads were roaming the city hanging on public lamp-posts any who might wish to follow the example of Field-Marshal Paulus and surrender to the Red Army. Brigades of boys from the *Hitlerjugend* were thrown practically unarmed into the street fighting. Hitler summoned up new forces from a supposed reserve he was keeping to the west of the city: the phantom 'Armee Wenck' that had long since been shot to pieces. There was no more petrol for the tanks and the city was under constant bombardment from Russian artillery. Within a week the Russians had fought their way to the centre of the city; the suburbs to the north and south were in their hands, and only to the west across the Tiergarten to the Grunewald was an escape route open.

On the 29th of April the *Führer* gathered his intimates and informed them solemnly that the end had come. Dönitz was to become *Führer*; he, Hitler, would die fighting at the head of his troops when the Russians came. For a moment the contact with reality had been restored. Then came the final plunge into the night of mythology. The myth of Frederick had failed him; but he remembered that Frederick had always carried poison with him for such an eventuality. The myth of the two Titans led to only one conclusion: the future belonged to the stronger nation. As for the German people: they had not proved worthy of their 'world-historical task', they had betrayed their *Führer*, they deserved the abyss. There remained the myth of the Nibelungen, the Teutonic myth of natural virtue and the corruption of gold, of loyalty and deceit, of passionate love and death transfigured. On the afternoon of the 30th of April, as the sound of Russian guns could be heard a few streets away, Hitler and Eva Braun took their lives—they had been married a few minutes before by a padre—she with poison, he with a revolver shot through the roof of the mouth. The corpses were hastily carried out and burnt in a shell crater in the Chancellery garden, where the charred remains were found by the Russians. Goebbels followed the example of his *Führer*, killing himself and his wife and children. The other inhabitants of the *bunker* fled to the West. Berlin surrendered to Marshal Zhukov. Over the remaining radio stations of the *Reich* the death of Adolf Hitler was made known to the strains of Siegfried's funeral march.

Chapter 12

GREAT BEAR AND LITTLE BEAR

1945-1948

REALLY Berlin had no right to survive at all. Bomber Harris and Joseph Stalin had hurled their *delendum est* at the city, and Mr. Secretary Morgenthau had wished it under the plough. At the last Hitler, too, had willed the destruction of his capital city: the vanquished deserve no quarter. And the mere volume of physical destruction, not to speak of the horror which had accompanied it, was reminiscent of Carthage or Nineveh. Whole streets, passageways and courtyards vanished under dunes of rubble over which the stumps of once distant steeples had become visible. It was now possible to see from Charlottenburg to Steglitz across the still flatter ruins of Wilmersdorf and Schöneberg. Fifty-seven per cent of the buildings in the city had been wrecked.

Not even the most fervent foreign admirers of Berlin had claimed in the past that she was beautiful; she was at her best a dowdy and old-fashioned, but infinitely good-natured aunt full of secrets and surprises for her protégés. The city did not offer motherly affection and understanding; she was too busy and matter-of-fact for such sentiments. And Berlin in its paternal aspect had tended to be all too Prussian for foreign tastes. But as an aunt Berlin was perfect: open-minded towards youth,

suspect to parents, making no demands, a slightly disreputable near relation of whom it was impossible not to be fond.
Thus, as an unshockable aunt—indeed far more likely to shock
you than let herself be shocked—Berlin had lived in her
Fräulein Schröders long after the Mr. Norrises and Herr
Issyvoos of the mad, gay 'twenties and barbarous 'thirties had
departed. Now her last vanities were gone. For eighteen months
and more the greater part of every day and night had been
spent in the cellar. On emerging after the all-clear another
block down the street, its large rooms stuffed with massive
Kaiser Wilhelm furniture, would be in flames. Towards the
end it was a matter of luck if the gas and water still worked;
windows were repaired only with cardboard. Through it all
Fräulein Schröder made her lugubrious comments on life
and preserved her practical good humour. Cockney toughness
and their sense of comedy kept the Berliners afloat.

The bombardment would play strange tricks. Notably un-
beautiful buildings would sometimes be improved; the profile of the ruined Memorial Church at the head of the Kurfürstendamm was pronounced a handsome addition to the city's
architecture. (This became an *idée fixe* with the Berliners.
Attempts to dismantle the ruin and build a modernistic substitute were frustrated as late as 1957 by a popular outcry. The
ruin had become an Ancient Monument.) Politics as such had
vanished; for the Fräulein Schröders it was a matter of keeping
body and soul together in this jungle of toppled masonry and
rusting girders. They waited for the Russians without emotion:
it might be better, it couldn't be worse. They might even have
welcomed the Red Army as liberators, had the would-be
liberators not made a major and uncharacteristic political
blunder.

The conduct of the Red Army in Berlin has been more
luridly described elsewhere. It is an ancient usage that the
womenfolk of the vanquished belong to the conqueror, and
the conduct of the other Allies and of the *Wehrmacht* itself in

occupied countries had no doubt left much to be desired. But it is really a question of orders. A modern army is not made up of mercenary *Landsknechte* like those from whom Berlin had suffered in the Thirty Years War. The order to plunder or not to plunder, to rape or not to rape is always issued at the highest level. The Nazis had given it deliberately in Poland and Russia—though not in France and Italy. In the Total State all human instincts are subject to the primacy of politics, and the humiliation of a people can well be political policy. Certainly little effort was made to hold the natural instincts of a sex-starved victorious army in check: '*es wurde fraternisiert*', as Brecht puts it sardonically in *Mother Courage*. It was, humanly speaking, a natural enough reaction to the miseries Hitler had inflicted on Russia. But it was a political mistake that was to cost the Russians dear.

Many would say that in these first few weeks of 'Liberation' —the Western Allies did not arrive until June—Stalin lost the game he was intending to play in Europe. For there is little doubt that Stalin meant to grab Germany, and more than Germany, if he could. The oldest joke in Eastern Europe is that '*mir*' means both 'peace' and 'world' in Russian, a fact which lends irony to the slogan 'The Soviet Union wants Peace', visible from Berlin to Vladivostock. Stalin, like Hitler, wanted the world; but, unlike Hitler, he had the gift of prudence. Just how strong Stalin's hand was in 1945 is not easy to assess. He had his ten-million-man army; but the Americans had the atom bomb. He had his Fifth Columns in every country in Europe; and in France and Italy Communist parties that had emerged from the Resistance with enormously increased prestige. Just how near the Soviet Union was to economic collapse, on the other hand, we shall probably never know; almost certainly Soviet morale would not have permitted another large-scale war. In the event, Stalin seemed unwilling to force things. A good Marxist, he waited for ripe fruits to fall.

And, according to Marxist-Leninist tradition, Germany

should have fallen first among the nations of Europe. Marx himself had thought so, and in the succeeding Internationals the German Social Democratic party had always had pride of place. During the 1920's the Bolsheviks had their direct wire to Berlin; it was not only Trotsky who expected an imminent outbreak of the proletarian revolution there. By 1932, the Communist party had increased its vote to six millions. So great was its self-confidence that it could reject common action with the Socialists against Hitler: indeed, Hitler could even be welcomed as the Antichrist whose coming should immediately precede the day of revolution. Only when it was too late for common action in Germany did the party launch its Popular Front against Fascism.

Yet the monstrous rule of Reaction in Germany could still be explained away dialectically on the principle 'the worse— the better': the worse things are now, the sooner they must mend. For the fundamental Marxist faith in the maturity of the German revolution remained untouched: Russia might be the mother of the revolution, but Germany was her eldest daughter, much as the French Church had been the eldest daughter of the Church of Rome. If Fascism was the most advanced stage of Capitalism, as was now proclaimed, then the revolution must follow immediately on its destruction. On the arrival of the Red Army, the German workers would seize power as they had done in November 1918, only this time the Red Army would be on the spot and would see to the consolidation of the power of the Soviets. The Americans, the British, and the French would soon accept a *fait accompli*, demobilize, and withdraw from Germany. The German revolution would at long last have come into its own and its capital would be—Berlin.

Why, then, did the ripe fruit fail to drop? For it did fail: the German revolution did not take place or even look like taking place. What the Russians established in their zone was not in the least revolutionary; it was State-Socialism-from-above or the old Prussian mixture-as-before. And the main reason was simply that revolutionary mood and spirit were lacking. The men were away from home, six millions killed or missing, millions more in Russia or—with better luck— in Western prison camps. Hundreds of thousands had been evacuated and those who remained had to think how they could feed their families and piece together their private worlds. The mood was one of exhaustion and total disillusionment. 'Politics has ruined us; politics is propaganda; propaganda is lies': this was not a mood in which revolution prospers.

The Russians were later to attribute their failure to Nazi indoctrination of the German people. But this was true only in one respect. Goebbels had prophesied rape and massacre and nobody had believed his cries of 'wolf-wolf'. Now the Russians had come and done their best to confirm this propaganda ('The little doctor was right after all', said the Berliners). It was impossible not to be impressed; perhaps Goebbels' prophecies of a collision between America and Russia would also come true? It was a case of wolves in wolves' clothing. The Kremlin was playing its hand with less than accustomed skill. In the summer of 1945 Stalin encouraged the Poles in the forcible expulsion of some eight million people from East Prussia, Pomerania, and Silesia: Hitler's racialism was being allowed to boomerang. (The Western Allies protested faintly at Potsdam that 'the expulsions should be carried out as humanely as possible'.) Marshal Zhukov put up posters in Berlin, proclaiming the eternal friendship of the Soviet people towards a democratic Germany; but the smash and grab went on regardless.

Overnight, thousands of skilled workers disappeared into the Soviet whale. Valuable pieces of electronic apparatus were dismantled at random from the Siemens factory and transported in cattle trucks to the Soviet Union (it was often beyond the skill of Soviet engineers to put the pieces together at the time; they appeared later on the world market in such unexpected places as Shanghai and Teheran). Telephones were gathered like grapes and loaded into open trucks with pitchforks. All the slumbering possessiveness of the peasant awoke in the Russian soldier, his appetite for wrist-watches was so insatiable he wore them from shoulder to wrist. The Berliners looked on amazed and helpless, and not without amusement. The West did not need to do much propaganda when the three occupying powers moved into their sectors of the city: the French in the north, the British in the central strip from the Brandenburger Tor to Spandau, and the Americans in the south from proletarian Neukölln to the middle-class strongholds of Zehlendorf and Dahlem. Neither quantity nor quality of sheep's clothing in subsequent years could disguise the wolf beneath the skin.

The expected Revolution had failed to occur. And not only the Revolution, the sudden explosion of creativity which had followed the collapse of 1918 failed to appear after 1945. Some good films were made in the DEFA studios in East Berlin: films about the war like *The Murderers are Among Us* by Wolfgang Staudte; but this time it was the Italians who made the most of their release from authoritarianism. The theatres in Berlin started up again with astonishing speed; new producers of talent came forward like Boleslav Barlog, Oscar Fritz Schuh, and Walter Felsenstein; but there was no explosion of new dramatic talent as in 1918. After 1945, it was Tennessee Williams, Anouilh and Giraudoux who became the staple diet of the once world-famed Berlin stage. (In 1948, admittedly, when the split between East and West was an established fact, the Eastern authorities offered the Schiffbauerdammtheater to Bertolt Brecht—but Brecht was no new figure, having made his name in Berlin at the very same theatre twenty years before.)

The younger generation, returning from the Eastern battlefields and the years behind barbed wire, were certainly as open to new ideas and as eager to express themselves as the young of 1918. The twelve years during which Germany had been cut off from European culture were quickly made good.

Sartre, Eliot, even Hemingway, Mayakovsky, and Proust were discovered for the first time. But apart from a mushroom growth of plays about returning soldiers and a few tortured war epics nothing of lasting value emerged. Why? Was it perhaps the very intensity and horror of the experience, combined with the hopelessness of the political outlook, that inhibited an adequate response? Ernst Toller had experienced the same horrors thirty years before, but his generation still had faith: faith in humanity in general and in revolution in particular. Who in post-1945 Berlin could look for the regeneration of humanity to hard-boiled Stalinist functionaries like Ulbricht and Pieck? After 1945, too, Germany was no longer mistress of her fate, nor for that matter was Berlin still her capital except in name. The Allies had not only taken over the political responsibility, but seen to it that Germany be deluged with propaganda whose tenor was that the Germans, after choosing Hitler, could never be trusted to choose a government again. This suited most people down to the ground. Few even bothered to answer these insinuations; the Berliners shrugged their shoulders and went back to their allotments.

If the younger generation, the generation which had grown up under the Nazis, was too shattered by its experience, the generation in between was all too conscious of the part it had played in bringing about the 'German catastrophe'. It was in fact the pre-Hitler generation that came to the rescue, the generation of Adenauer and Heuss and Schumacher, many of whom had come to maturity before the First World War. Among writers it was Gottfried Benn, the sensation of literary Berlin in 1910, who found his voice again in the grey, disillusioned post-Expressionist Berlin of 1947. Though a highly esoteric writer, he reflects well enough the ambiguous attitude of many Berliners of his class and generation. Benn was one of the few writers who had stayed in Germany after Hitler's coming to power. In 1938 he was forbidden to publish and went back to the army as a medical officer: 'The Army has become', he wrote, 'the only respectable form of emigration.' But among the rootless literati and garrulous Jewish intelligentsia of the Berlin Twenties, Benn had always cut an extremely Prussian figure.

The son of a pastor in the March, he had received his training in the Royal Military School of Medicine. With the young T. S. Eliot Benn believed that poets should look like bank clerks, however deep they may delve into the pit of human corruption. This attitude is reflected in his poetry. He used for his early verse the colourful and drastic language of medical students: but the forms remained strict. He liked, in his writing, to imagine himself the impassive surgeon he was in his professional life; a surgeon does not require an abstract faith in humanity to perform his duty. And such was Benn's *Doppelleben* (so reminiscent of E. T. A. Hoffmann's): by day the Prussian officer, all duty and honour and stiff upper lip; by night the artist pariah, sworn Nihilist and Nietzschean. In his *Berliner Novelle* (1947) he writes of the patients in his surgery for whom 'in the unheated rooms at a temperature of minus 10° C., the withdrawal of an arm from its covering rags could lead to fresh pathological symptoms. . . . My business was at a standstill and I was glad. I was at last alone. Unable to stand the thumping and jingling at the front door any longer, I mounted a machine gun that I had rescued with some pains from the international slaughter, to cover the approaches and pop off any suspicious characters. The corpses did not look any different from those that had died of exposure or finished off the job themselves; they lay about on the pavement and the passers-by thought nothing of it. . . .'

Benn had always been a specialist in gallows' humour, and now was the occasion for it. As a doctor, certainly, he was prepared to treat any patients who might come to him: but as an artist he was an avowed enemy of the human race. Raskolnikov, he remarks, murdered an old woman and—who would believe it?—felt the need to suffer and be forgiven. But that was

M

seventy years ago; who, in our time, would dream of applying ethical criteria to mortality statistics? 'In a world in which
such atrocities occur, in which indeed atrocities are the accepted
norm, it is a matter of indifference whether a few human beings
live a few days longer or sleep a few nights more. . . . Away with
this confused babble about life and happiness. Matter is radia-
tion, and God is silence, and what comes in between is so much
offal.' As to a release from the *Doppelleben* of our time: 'the
next century will permit only two human types: those who
choose a life of action, who want to get on in the world, and
those who await in silence the metamorphosis of matter—
criminals and monks, nothing else will be feasible'. And as for
political action—'what self-respecting man would make a
public stand for anything like that today? . . . History! The
well-nourished sit in the stalls with their concubines and favourites, and the violins entertain the murderers to sweet music.
In the dark the anonymous victims sink down. . . . There is
nothing to protest against here, to make a stand about, not
with the small sling and not with the big drum: let them drive
their chariots over the bones of the dead!'

Benn is, of course, writing of the Nazis. And yet not only
of the Nazis. One army is like another; the sack of Berlin like
the sack of Rome; orders are orders; slaughter is slaughter.
Has not the artist as much right to defend his private world
with a machine gun as the fat men in the stalls with their
slogans of Total War and Unconditional Surrender? In a world
without demonstrable historical or metaphysical meaning, has
not the artist as much right to defend his private meaning as
the capitalists and the commissars?

Benn liked to call himself a *phenotype*. He had no ambition,
he declared, to express anything other than what he and his
generation had experienced. The artist is no prophet, no interpreter, he lives like other men in the grey world of phenomena. He knows nothing of any *genotype*, of any unalterable
'human nature', of historical inevitability, of Christian or

Western values: history is an invention of clerks who have sold themselves to the commissars and cardinals. Benn considered himself the *phenotype* of the faithless, rootless city-dweller of the mid-twentieth century, and indeed specifically of post-1945 Berlin. Benn would have been the last to deny that his pessimistic utterances were conditioned by his environment. 'On the boulevards the overspill of the steppes, vigorous brothel business, uniforms everywhere. The bars fill up again with customers from Siberia and Hawaii. White Vodka, grey Whisky; Ayala and Cliquot from unwashed tumblers. Comrades and Gentlemen sway on the red glass floor, the population watching greedily through the windows: culture is on the move again, fewer murders, more songs and noise! Even the inner life of the defeated is well cared for: a trans-atlantic bishop arrives, and simpers "Dearly beloved brethren"; a humanist makes his appearance, and flutes "Western Civilization"; a tenor wheedles "*O holde Kunst*". The rehabilitation of Europe has begun.' There is, of course, a strain of resentment in this that was not part of Benn's intention. He wished for no protest. The new masters from Hawaii and Turkestan were neither better nor worse than the former owners. And if it was pointed out to him that the former owners had forbidden him to publish, he could have replied in kind—for the Allies had his name on their black list as a Nazi for many years after the war. But Benn did not protest. He was a *phenotype*, and the phenotypical Berliner of 1947 wanted nothing so much as to be left alone. Better an unresolved *Doppelleben* than the life of a cog in the totalitarian machine.

Chapter 13

A TALE OF TWO CITIES

1948–1958

YET the Berliners were not to be left alone, any more than the other war-weary peoples of Europe. The first blows in a new world conflict were to fall on their city. Berlin, wrecked and depopulated as she was, still remained the European power-pivot she had been from the time of the Seven Years War, when the city had seen Russian soldiers for the first time. Quite apart from the significance to Communist sentiment of the city of Hegel and Marx and Lassalle and Liebknecht, Berlin was crucial to Russian strategy. As long as the Western powers had a foothold in Berlin, the consolidation of a Communist regime was impossible. It was soon obvious that if the cake were to be divided between the Allies, contrary to the proclamations of the Big Four at Potsdam in the summer of 1945, then the Russians would get the largest slice, but the slice poorest in currants.

Only Berlin itself, and industrial Saxony in the south, possessed anything like a class-conscious proletariat. Yet without that Ulbricht and his men must be reduced to puppets of Marshal Zhukov. In other ways, too, the Soviet Zone was not promising. Brandenburg, Mecklenburg, and Pomerania had been the provinces on which Bismarck had once relied for his reactionary majorities, and were in 1945 still on a very low rung of the historical dialectic. The *Junkers* could be forcibly expropriated; but an agrarian country could not be industrialized overnight, or indeed industrialized at all as long as the dismantlement and reparations policy continued. Saxony was the only plum, with its uranium ore, precision engineering, and plentiful soft coal. There at least Communism had deep roots; and Leipzig, Dresden, and Chemnitz (renamed Karl-Marx-Stadt) could be insulated without difficulty from the West. But both in industrial Saxony and in Berlin (still the largest industrial city in Germany) there was a snag—these areas were also the traditional strongholds of the SPD. With Berlin it might be possible to build up a People's Democracy within the Soviet Zone, but without the co-operation of the SPD not even the loyalty of the workers could be counted upon. Stalin needed velvet gloves for the operation.

The earlier history of attempts at Socialist unity had been a truly tragic one, in Berlin as in the rest of Europe. From the day in August 1914, when the majority of the SPD voted the War Credits, the movement had been split between the followers of Scheidemann and Ebert and the radical descendants of Karl Liebknecht and Rosa Luxemburg. After Ebert's appeal to the *Freikorps* to put down the Spartacist rising in January 1919, it had become an irreconcilable antagonism. The gap steadily widened during the years of the Weimar Republic. The Socialists were accused of having compromised with the *bourgeois* Establishment and the Communists of irresponsible subversion. Nothing was forgiven and forgotten; Spartacus and its bloody end stood between the SPD and the KPD.

What happened in Ernst Reuter's Berlin after 1945 had its roots in the Berlin of 1919. Ernst Reuter himself had taken part in the struggle and been compelled to make his choice. At twenty-five, as a young Social Democrat, he had opposed the granting of the War Credits. At twenty-nine he had been made commissar for Volga German affairs by the Bolsheviks and had brought back with him to Berlin a letter of recommendation from Lenin to the German Communists. Within a few months the able young man had become General Secretary of the KPD. Yet a short time later he had broken with the party and its methods and begun to work on the Social Democratic paper *Vorwärts*. Reuter was the son of a Prussian official and himself an extremely competent administrator. In the late 'twenties he had created the *Berliner Verkehrsgesellschaft*—the counterpart of the London Passenger Transport Board—unifying the overhead and underground railways and the bus system of Berlin. In 1932 he was elected to the *Reichstag*, and, in the following year, twice thrown by the Nazis into a concentration camp for his Socialist activities. His years of forced emigration were spent in Ankara as a lecturer in Political Science. After 1945, he returned to his old work in the Berlin administration, and, in 1947, was elected Lord Mayor of the city, after the shattering defeat of the Russians' party in the only free post-war elections to take place in all four sectors of Berlin. But the Soviets had not forgotten his past. Lenin's letter of recommendation still rankled. They persuaded the Western allies not to recognize Reuter as Lord Mayor.

Meanwhile the Russians had organized their Socialist Unity Party, the SED, which was to become, in Walter Ulbricht's hands, the instrument of Soviet domination in the later 'German Democratic Republic'. Superficially the Russians appeared to have a strong hand. They could argue that Socialist disunity had paved the way for Hitler's triumphs. They could build to some extent on the comradeship in suffering of Communists and Socialists in the concentration camps and the resistance movement. And, above all, they had the argument of power. The German Right was shattered; under the benevolent wing of the Soviet occupying power a Socialist revolution could be carried through, if only Socialists could agree to work together. The Russians still held the initiative. It was they who had defeated Fascism and hunted down Hitler to his lair. The returned Muscovites with Ulbricht and Pieck knew exactly what they wanted. They had arrived literally in the baggage of the Red Army and were ready to take orders from the Soviet military commander. Their original plan to revive the old KPD was soon dropped, and another was concocted requiring a delicacy they can have had little opportunity to practise during their years in Moscow: they must woo the Social Democrats into the SED.

This operation was attempted in the Russian headquarters in Karlshorst during the late summer of 1946 in circumstances of considerable obscurity. And the results were negative. Otto Grotewohl and a handful of Social Democrats declared themselves willing to work with the Communists; the majority under Franz Neumann refused to be stampeded and decided to fight the election alone. Much to the chagrin of the Russians the SPD won over fifty per cent of the votes and the SED only about twenty per cent. But though the first round had been lost, the Russians could afford to wait. In the Eastern Zone itself, where they could do as they wished, every conceivable pressure was put on the Social Democrats to throw in their lot with the SED; the party cadres in Saxony and elsewhere were reorganized and consolidated under Walter Ulbricht.

In Berlin, the Russians tried the iron fist and the velvet glove alternately. Excellent cultural officers such as the legendary Colonel Tulpanov, who is said to have spoken ten languages, were appointed; and much was done for the cultural, and particularly for the theatrical life of the city. Up to 1948, the four sectors of the city still had a common theatrical and musical life: the Russians brought their star violinists and ballerinas to compete with the culture of the West. The French set up their *Maison de France*, the Americans their *Amerikahaus*, and the British their British Centre. It seemed for a time as if Berlin might still reap the fruits and not only the thorns of the East-West conflict.

But with 1948 came the *annus fatalis* of Stalinism. Czechoslovakia slipped behind the Iron Curtain; Jan Masaryk died, Stalin decided that accounts must be settled. Tito had received his ultimatum a year before, dared to oppose, and had been outlawed by the newly founded Cominform. In France, the great strikes of the autumn of 1947 had been unsuccessful. In Italy the situation was still critical. Elections in the Western Zones of Germany and in Berlin herself had made it plain that Germany was not to be won by playing the democratic game. But to create a viable Communist state in the Soviet Zone meant the inclusion of Berlin; by hook or by crook the Western Allies must be pushed out of the city.

The first attempts to turn the Berliners against the Western Allies had failed. They merely served to heal the breach between victor and vanquished in the Western sectors and raise Western suspicions as to Russian good faith. The Western Allies must be quickly squeezed out and Berlin follow Prague into the Eastern camp. At the beginning of 1948, Russian coal deliveries stopped; thousands of Berliners were brought to hospitals suffering from frost-bite and exposure. On the 24th of January the coaches for German civilians were detached from the Allied military trains; Berliners could no longer travel freely to the West. Then, on the 23rd of June, three days after the crucial introduction of a currency reform in Western Germany, all goods and passenger transport to Western Germany was cut off: the bridge over the Elbe being 'temporarily closed to all traffic on account of repairs'. The blockade had begun.

At first the significance of the Soviet action was not fully appreciated; the rest of Europe, and particularly Western Germany, had too many problems of her own. It was the Americans who, as in the days of the Korean crisis, grasped the situation and succeeded in wrenching the initiative from the hands of the Soviets. An American journalist observed at the time: 'If Berlin is abandoned, half Europe will be in the Communist party tomorrow.' Stalin had thrown down the gauntlet to the Western powers. More than Allied prestige was at stake, the myth of the Russian steam-roller must be destroyed or Europe would go to pieces without a struggle.

It is the more remarkable that the decision was made not in Washington, but by the man on the spot, General Lucius D. Clay. And a lightning decision was needed. Unless transport was improvised, Berlin would be starving in a matter of days; industry would have to close down and the Allies themselves would be compelled to withdraw. The alternatives were to force supplies through to Berlin under armed escort—which might well have led to world war—or to use the air corridors to fly in supplies from the West. General Clay decided on his own authority to start at once with an air shuttle service between Berlin and the American Air Command at Wiesbaden. Only a month later did he go to Washington and obtain permission to fly in some four thousand five hundred tons of food and fuel and raw material a day. The British and French authorities followed the American initiative; in addition to Tempelhof airfield in the American sector, Tegel in the French sector, and Gatow (the RAF's 'piece of cake') in the British sector were open to the Air Lift. C54's were brought in from Alaska, Panama, and Hawaii, and the amount of material flown in rose to a record of thirteen thousand tons in a single day.

For the Berliners it was a strange sight. Only four years previously the planes that were now bringing them the necessities of life had showered destruction on their city. They christened them the '*Rosinenbomber*', 'currant bombers'. The mistrust and resentment against the Western Allies vanished overnight, in Berlin and in Western Germany the mood changed from sullen resignation to willing co-operation. The Air Lift and the Marshall Plan had succeeded where a thousand goodwill conferences might have failed. The German people threw in their lot wholeheartedly with the West.

It is strange that Stalin had not foreseen this; or had he already despaired of the carrot and resolved on the stick? Certainly his bluff was easily called. The Russians seemed stunned by the efficiency and sheer material effort of the Air Lift; giving, as it did, a peaceful exhibition of America's stupendous war potential. Very little effort at interference was made. When the French blew up the Soviet-owned radio tower near Tegel airport in the face of most dire threats, the Communists hoped for a strong Russian reaction. But in fact nothing happened, the Soviets accepted the affront and kept quiet. The Russians varied their tactics. Meat and vegetables were offered at cheap prices in the shops of East Berlin. An Eastern Mark was introduced; but the Berliners did not accept it at the same value as the 'Westmark'. They were not to be tempted. Ernst Reuter now became the interpreter of the new mood of defiance. When Communist rowdies broke into the municipal assembly (reminiscent of the last free session of the *Reichstag* when the Social Democrats had voted against Hitler in the presence of armed storm-troopers), the non-Communist parties withdrew and moved over to West Berlin. There, in Schöneberg Town Hall, Ernst Reuter was at last recognized by the Western Allies as acting Lord Mayor of Berlin.

The city was now openly split into two political and administrative halves. The Soviet East Sector had the immediate advantage: the old centre of Berlin, the site of the first settlements on the banks of the Spree, with Unter den Linden, the Wilhelmstrasse and the ruins of the Royal Palace. (This was blown up to make room for a platform from which Ulbricht and Grotewohl could take the salute at May Day demonstrations.) The East had the Town Hall and the other administrative buildings and could claim to be the legitimate successor to the municipality of Greater Berlin. East Berlin even had Fritz Ebert, the son of the former President, as Lord Mayor. The West, though with a population of two and a quarter million to East Berlin's one million, lacked a clearly defined centre; the

The Siemens plant.
West Berlin at work . . .

CITY LIGHTS

. . . and at play.
Kurfurstendamm with memorial church.

The poet Gottfried
Benn (1886–1956)

(*Ullstein-Eschen*)

. . . prophet of doom

. . . and of hope

Ernst Reuter,
the Bear's Champion
(Mayor,
1948–1953)

American encampment was way out at Dahlem, and Schöne-berg, the centre of the new city government, was merely one borough among many. Eventually, the area between the Zoo station and the Kurfürstendamm became the new focus of life in West Berlin, dominated by the ragged profile of the Memorial Church.

To the real Berliner the Kurfürstendamm had seemed, ever since the Twenties, more intimately '*berlinisch*' than the old city based on the Friedrichstrasse and Unter den Linden. The latter were for the tourists from the rest of Germany and for the foreigners. They belonged to the *Reich*, rather than to Berlin proper. There arose a mystique of the bracing *Berliner Luft* and *Berliner Tempo*; the Berliners liked to think of themselves as Goethe's 'verwegener Menschenschlag'—a gay, defiant race of desperadoes. This mystique was linked with the Romanisches Café near the Memorial Church and with the promenading *demi-monde* of the Kurfürstendamm and its back-street dives: 'Wild West Berlin' as the catch-phrase had it. Now the shat-tered tower of the Memorial Church had become a symbol of the Berliners' defiance of the new tyranny from the East. Ernst Reuter hit the world's headlines overnight. The Bear awoke from his slumbers.

Like many great Berliners, Ernst Reuter was not born in the city. But he had come to it as a young man, and the Berliners are ready to overlook accidents of birth in taking a man to their hearts. For Reuter was a born tribune of the people. His humour and personal warmth gave him a popular touch that few German Socialist leaders have had. Like Kurt Schumacher, the other great personality of the post-war SPD, he made free use of the rhetoric of political freedom, but he had nothing of the fanatic and only a little of the demagogue about him. Reuter resembled Roosevelt, more than any other modern leader, in his ability to understand the mood of the people and give it expression. Like Roosevelt he knew how to speak directly to the masses without exciting their hysteria; his weekly talks to the West Berliners over the radio made the same direct, personal appeal as F.D.R.'s fireside talks had done. And, consciously or unconsciously, Ernst Reuter set about creating a myth: the myth of Berlin as the predestined outpost of Western Freedom and Civilization.

The Bear, as we have seen, had been politically inarticulate in the past despite the Berliners' natural eloquence and despite the early growth of revolutionary parties. Frederick the Great had said: 'They can say what they like, as long as they let me do what I like.' '*Berliner Schnauze*' had come to mean 'shooting your mouth off': the authorities did not like the sound of it but they knew it to be harmless. The Bear had muttered and growled and been uncomfortably conscious of the Eagle on his broad back. But no revolution had ever succeeded in Berlin; the Bear was altogether too good-natured, and genuine revolutions are the product of hatred and despair.

Now for the first time the Bear had found a voice to express his defiance. The old eagles were gone. The Bear had the chance to stand on his hind legs and had to learn to do so quickly if he was not to succumb to the new tyranny from outside. Ernst Reuter, wearing his perpetual beret at a jaunty angle and driving to Schöneberg Town Hall every day in his Volkswagen, appealed to the Berliners' instinctive distrust of power: and no people had had better opportunity to develop this instinct than the former subjects of the King of Prussia. Now Prussia had been dissolved by Allied proclamation and the majority of the old ruling class had been killed or fled to West Germany. Berlin was more than ever a proletarian city, and the Berlin worker had too sharp a political instinct not to detect in Stalinism the mixture-as-before. Reuter had rejected this same creed for himself twenty-five years earlier and had decided to work for a democratic Socialism in Germany. It was to a deep-rooted democratic instinct in the Berliners that he made his appeal.

The Air Lift was the watershed of post-1945 Berlin. From

Frohnau in the north, down through the centre of the city, and then away to the south-east between Treptow and Neukölln, the People's Police erected street barriers and guard posts. There were now two currencies, two Town Halls, two Lord Mayors, two Police Forces: and neither authority recognized the other. Chaos was forestalled, however, by convenient make-believe. Telephone connections were severed, but every day a rickety yellow mail-van lumbered through the Brandenburger Tor bringing letters from one half of Berlin to the other. The overhead railway (*S-Bahn*), run by the Eastern authorities, and the underground (*U-Bahn*), run by the West, continued to function. Workers had to be brought to factories in the East from their Western homes in Wedding or Neukölln. The two Police Forces continued to exchange information about criminals supposed to have fled from one sector to another (and Berlin had long been living in the world of the *Third Man* and *The Threepenny Opera*). Actors who had previously worked for theatres and film studios in both East and West were now put under pressure to determine their political allegiance. Those who left the East did so as often as not from political conviction. Communism had lost its initiative and in West Berlin there was the concrete fact of political and artistic freedom. The Western world was rediscovering its own much-trumpeted values.

Inevitably the University became a focus of conflict. The old university Wilhelm von Humboldt had founded in 1810 still stood on Unter den Linden and the Communists were quick to exploit the fact that it lay within their territorial power. During the Air Lift the situation became acute, and it was the students who made the first move. They decided to found a new 'Free University' in West Berlin and persuade the non-Communist teaching staff to move in a body from the venerable buildings on Unter den Linden to new pastures in the Kaiser Wilhelm Scientific Institutes in American-occupied Dahlem (where Professor Hahn had split the atom ten years

before). The enterprise succeeded. It seemed for a moment as
if the liberal idealism of Wilhelm von Humboldt were reborn;
the Humboldt who had written his *Boundaries of the State's
Activities* as a young student of Kant, and resigned from the
Prussian service in 1819 in protest against the King's reactionary
policies. Another Prussian liberal of the old school, the historian Friedrich Meinecke, offered, at the age of eighty-eight,
to become the first rector of the Free University. Meinecke
had published his *German Catastrophe* shortly before, the most
courageous and most personal of all revaluations of the German
past after the collapse of 1945. The young men who had come
back from the war and who remembered Nazism were not
likely to fall for totalitarianism as their parents had done, and
Meinecke, intimate with the men of the 20th of July, had
fought the Nazi version as well as the Soviet. Meinecke was the
last of the great line of Berlin historians: Niebuhr and Ranke,
Treitschke and Droysen, Mommsen, Troeltsch and Del-
brück. The Eastern University might call itself the 'Humboldt
Universität', but the infant 'Freie Universität' could boast the
true spiritual descent from Wilhelm von Humboldt.

In certain respects, then, Berlin did reap the fruits and not
the thorns of its position as a power-pivot between East and
West. Duplication could mean enrichment. The city now had
three opera houses and a dozen theatres, both sides being
anxious to use their sectors as window-dressing for their way
of life. The East rebuilt the old Frankfurter Allee, renamed
Stalinallee, in best Muscovite 'pastry-cook style'. The West,
with generous American aid, replanted the devastated Tiergarten and built the new Free University a home near the
American HQ among the sedate villas of Dahlem. In May
1949, less than a year after it began, the Soviets raised the
blockade, silently and mysteriously, without explanation or
apology. In accordance with the Leninist maxim that 'Communists must know how to retreat', they called off an action
that had cost them dear: cost them all hope of bringing

Germany into their camp and alerted the rest of Europe to Stalin's aims.

The Air Lift had focused the attention of the world on Berlin; and Berlin has always thrived on attention. It is, perhaps, her one feminine trait. But the realities of political warfare were not always favourable to cultural and economic life. The Eastern Zone had suffered from the Western counter-blockade of coal and raw materials, and the natural poverty of the Soviet slice of the cake became quickly apparent. The highly industrialized West, on the other hand, had responded to the tonic effects of Marshall Aid, and isolated Berlin soon found herself lagging behind. The newly-founded Federal Republic instituted an emergency levy, two *pfennigs* a postage stamp, for the capital of the *Reich*. Old feelings of animosity had now been replaced by admiration for the Berliners' toughness and humour in adversity.

For there were dangers and disadvantages enough in Berlin's front-line position. Outspoken anti-Communists could be kidnapped and smuggled to East Berlin. Heavy sentences were common for political crimes on both sides of the Iron Curtain. It was impossible for West Berliners to spend their week-ends in the countryside: a certain claustrophobia added to the political tension. Both sides consolidated their fronts and their definitions of loyalty until, in 1954, Otto John's crossing of a street from one half of Berlin to the other could be construed as high treason. But the most prominent and controversial *Grenzgänger* ('border-dodger') was Bertolt Brecht whose decision to accept the offer of the East German government to set up his experimental theatre in East Berlin became inevitably a cause of political scandal. Brecht's life and work, like Benn's, was so intimately connected with the Berlin of these years that it is worth making a closer inspection.

Brecht's last action as an exile in America had been to swear before the Un-American Activities Committee that he had never been a member of the Communist party. This was a white lie. It was true that he had never held a party card. Those who knew his Mother Courage, his Azdak or Galileo knew how firmly he had his tongue in his cheek; those who did not, called him a liar. The latter were not surprised when he accepted the Communist offer: but then nor were the former. Brecht was no less crafty than his favourite characters; if the regime was capable of exploiting him, he was also quite capable of exploiting the regime. Berlin had been the scene of his early triumphs. The idea of 'Epic Theatre' had emerged from the experimentation of the Twenties in Berlin, particularly from Piscator's Proletarian Theatre on the Nollendorfplatz. There is a legend that Max Reinhardt, virtual dictator of theatrical taste in Berlin before 1914, sat in on the rehearsals of Brecht's early play *Drums in the Night*, and having watched the youthful Brecht producing, left the theatre without a word. The old spellbinder had sensed his match—and his deadliest adversary.

Like young Spitta in Gerhart Hauptmann's *The Rats*, 1912, Brecht hated all the pathos and mystification and idealism of the traditional German theatre. He hated 'spellbinding'. The times were evil: people should not be allowed to forget this in the theatre, it must be hammered into them and they must be persuaded to change the society they live in. Down with all spellbinding and all kowtowing to *Kultur*! But Brecht did not make much progress. Aestheticism and German worship of *Kultur* went too deep, and the otherwise very lively theatre of the Nazi period brought a return to the hated 'culinary' opera and heroic tragedy in the style of *Götz von Berlichingen*.

Brecht, like the young Marx in Berlin in 1840, was in full revolt against the 'German Ideology', that Idealism which connives at the human wish to ignore the world as it is. Brecht's Materialism was the angry insistence of an intellectual on the forgotten fundamentals of human life. His plays were full of talk of eating and drinking: 'First mind your belly and then mind your morals', runs a famous refrain in *The Threepenny Opera*. He wanted to drive home Marx's 'presupposition which is the presupposition of human existence. . . . I mean, that men must have the wherewithal to live before they can make history. To live, however, it is first necessary to eat and drink. . . .' The clumsiness of the sarcasm may be un-Brechtian, but the basic contention is the same.

Brecht's return to East Berlin was an event. He was not only the most gifted playwright and producer Germany possessed and successor to the great Berlin tradition of Iffland, Otto Brahm, and Max Reinhardt, he was also the only major writer in the Western world to have remained a Communist. Like W. H. Auden, he had been attracted to Marxism in his 'twenties by its discipline and rationality, but unlike Auden, Spender, Gide and Malraux he had struck roots in what most Western intellectuals were soon to find distinctly alien soil. There was nothing amateurish or smarty about Brecht's Marxism. He was a Central European familiar with the ways of the Hegelian dialectic and prepared to follow the Marxist argument to its radical conclusion. Yet Brecht never joined the party. The West watched intently, and vainly, for the first signs of discontent with the regime. Did Brecht approve of the forced Stalinization, the reopened concentration camps, and above all the putting down of the rising of June 1953 by Russian tanks? There is evidence to suggest that Brecht did disapprove, but he had made his bargain. His situation was that of his own Galileo Galilei, or indeed of any writer in a non-liberal society.

And Brecht was certainly as little of a Liberal as his fellow-poet in the other half of the city, Gottfried Benn. (The two together make an interesting pair, Gog and Magog of a divided culture. Their views of poetry are curiously complementary: Benn with his lyrical subjectivity, Brecht with his 'epic' objectivity.) Liberalism, even of Humboldt's variety, was another form of Idealism, another false heroism. Liberalism is for those who can afford it! The philosophy of Mother Courage, of Azdak, and of Galileo is that wisdom consists in

N

non-exposure, in not being noticed by the powers of this world, in living close to the ground, uncommitted and ready for compromise with life. 'I will do no one the favour of displaying human dignity', cries Azdak, when the days of revolution are over and the soldiers strip him of his judge's robe. This aspect of Brecht's philosophy was certain to offend those in power sooner or later. Thus when his opera *Lucullus* was performed in 1951 for the first time, he was compelled to withdraw it for Marxist self-criticism and revision. The party bosses considered it too negative, too pacifist: the Phrygian King who resisted Lucullus ought to have been presented as the patriotic defender of his country against Roman imperialism. They must have realized dimly, too, that Brecht's mockery could be directed against them.

Nevertheless, Brecht's productions at his grubby Theater am Schiffbauerdamm continued to outshine anything that the West could offer in the other half of the city. Berlin had become once again a place of artistic pilgrimage. After Brecht's death in the summer of 1956, his *Life of Galilei* was performed at the Theater am Schiffbauerdamm for the first time. Here Brecht seemed to have painted a self-portrait, and yet one of strange ambiguity. Galileo, too, lived in a non-liberal society and recanted his heretical views. In his notes to the play Brecht makes his condemnation of Galileo quite clear; by his cowardice he has betrayed his friends, his science, and human progress. What can be said in his defence? In the play itself Andrea del Sarto, Galileo's pupil, who has previously condemned his action, provides a defence of his recantation when Galileo hands him his '*Discorsi*', the secretly composed fruit of his retirement. 'Galileo was craftier than all of us', he declares. 'He made an outward act of surrender and continued secretly with his great work of Enlightenment!' But Galileo, now an old man, says only: 'They showed me the instruments of torture. I was afraid of physical pain', and turns back to his food. Brecht was equivocal to the last. We do not know whether or not to accept Galileo's apology from the mouth of Andrea del Sarto, and Brecht's death in August 1956 robbed us of the possibility of knowing. But among Brecht's last observations is said to have been the cryptic: 'Even after my death there will be opportunities for making trouble.' It was the remark of a man who knew his way about the modern world of violence and propaganda. Would it be wrong to add: of a true Berliner, a lifelong ally of the Bear against the Eagle of oppression?

N*

POSTSCRIPT

1959

A LINE drawn on the map of Europe from Paris to Moscow passes through Berlin. Paris is the nearer city; but the East is more generous with time and space. For all practical purposes Berlin is the midway point between the capital of world Communism and the undeclared capital city of the West. We have tried to show that Berlin has held its thankless position as Europe's power-pivot since about the beginning of the eighteenth century; since, that is to say, the emergence of Russia as a European power. Before that Berlin had been a provincial outpost on the ragged north-eastern frontier of the Empire; it was at Vienna that the lines of force met and contended. Before that, the Eastern power for centuries had been not Russia, but Turkey; and Vienna lay approximately half-way between Paris and Constantinople.

But the rise of Prussia and Russia is only a part of a more general shift of power, particularly economic power, to the countries of Northern Europe. After 1700, Spain, Italy, and even Austria are on the downward slope. The new world powers come from the north: Russia, England, and Germany under the leadership of Prussia. France alone keeps her place in the balance of power before and after 1700—only to lose it with the general decline of European influence in the world.

But by this time England and Germany too, exhausted by mutual wars, had sunk to the rank of minor European—minor because European—powers in the world at large.

But this was not to be the end of the story. For if in 1945 Europe ceased to be the world's arbiter, she remained the world's battleground. When the post-war struggle for power in Europe—in the guise of an ideological war between East and West—began, Germany inevitably became the most coveted prize. We have suggested in a previous chapter that Stalin was very confident of his success. The game of politics seemed to prescribe that a reactionary regime must be followed by revolution of the Left. Germany seemed to be in the bag: the 'Ami's' would 'go home'; by hook or by crook the Socialists would be induced to co-operate; and a 'cold revolution', as in Prague, would be carried through as rapidly and efficiently as possible. After that, with German industrial potential in Stalin's hands, France and England could be granted the token neutrality of a Finland or an Austria.

It will long be a matter of debate just why this did not happen. Did America foresee the economic consequences of a new period of isolationism? Or did Europe shake off its slumbers before it was too late? It is too soon to see the Truman Era in perspective, and the decision to regard the zonal frontier across Germany as America's Eastern front against Communism may not have been the work of any one man. Yet the stages on the way are clear enough: the Marshall Plan, the *coup d'état* in Prague, the civil war in Greece, the Italian elections, and, not least, the Berlin Air Lift. The Korean war put the finishing touches to the design with American insistence on the rearmament of Western Germany.

But the Korean war was significant in another way. The momentum of Communist expansion had now passed to the Far East: to China, Korea, and Viet-Nam. In the West, the Communists had already lost the initiative. This process, which had started with the isolation of the Communist parties in

France and Italy, was accelerated by the Berlin blockade and
the subsequent Allied counter-blockade of the Russian zone
of Germany. But we should be careful not to over-dramatize
the Berlin blockade. It was perhaps more important for its
impact on the West than as a demonstration to the Communist
world. Even after their humiliating climb-down, the Soviets
seemed to succeed for a while in winning the younger generation in the Soviet Zone for Communism. In the summer of
1951, the World Youth Festival, with its thousands of blue-
shirted youths and maidens chanting '*Freundschaft*' through
the streets of East Berlin, was an impressive demonstration of
Communist strength, unshaken by the Korean war or the set-
backs in Western Europe.

It was in fact only gradually that the tide began to turn
against the East, and it was not so much the libertarian ideology
of the West as its growing economic strength that did the
trick. The 'economic miracle' that Marshall Aid had brought
about in Western Germany meant full employment and high
wages in the Ruhr. In a few years West Germany had reached
and surpassed her pre-war export records, while in East Germany the Russians were still draining the economy with their
reparation demands. A second mass flight of population from
East Germany began; between 1948 and 1958 over two million people fled from the Soviet zone to the West.

It would be wrong to regard all these people as choosers of
freedom, as 'ideological' refugees. Perhaps the majority were
what are unkindly known in Germany as '*Konjunkturritter*'
—'boom-jockeys'. But this is to see the problem in a false
light. If the artificial frontier between East and West Germany
had not existed, these people would not have been refugees at
all; they would have been simply making use of their freedom
to change their place of work. For nearly a century there had
been a recognized drift away from the backward Eastern territories towards the West—towards emigration to America or
absorption in the industries of the Ruhr valley. It was part of a

long-term westward migration of European labour, akin to the westward drift of European Jewry.

Outwardly, however, the Communist regime of Grotewohl and Ulbricht seemed unshaken. Indeed the conviction that no resistance against a totalitarian state is possible from within was so deeply rooted that the rising of the 17th of June 1953 took the West unawares. Yet seen in the perspective of even one decade, it is clear that such explosions are quite possible; what is impossible is that they can lead to success when the government has a modern army at its beck and call, as Ulbricht had in 1953 and Kadar in 1956. The story of the 17th of June is significant enough, though it is now dwarfed by the bloodier events of the autumn of 1956 in Budapest.

The building workers engaged in erecting the neo-Muscovite pomp of the Stalinallee had refused to accept the higher norms dictated to them from above. With no very sinister purpose they marched to the city centre to demonstrate in front of the government buildings. On the way they were joined by workers from other factories in East Berlin. Members of the government made their appearance and hastily promised reduction of the norms. In response to shouts from the crowd, other vague promises of reform were given. But the crowds gathering in the streets of the old city quickly grew bolder in the general anonymity. Newspaper stalls were set on fire, cars overturned, slogans torn down. Finally the crowd made for the Brandenburger Tor itself, two young men shinned up a pole and successfully hauled down the red flag, the symbol of Ulbricht's power in East Berlin. The lid was off. In some instances the People's Police attacked the demonstrators, in others they held back and appeared to be in sympathy; the rioters were after all 'fellow-workers'. Later in the afternoon two Soviet armoured divisions were thrown into the city to clear the streets. At several points demonstrators started to pelt the oncoming tanks with stones and in the ensuing struggle sixteen Berliners were killed. Nevertheless, the display of force succeeded in its purpose. The demonstrators were dispersed. Berlin had witnessed yet another abortive revolution.

It was in the Eastern Zone itself, however, that the main explosion took place. As soon as the news of the Berlin demonstrations came through, people began to collect in the streets and in front of the Town Halls of the towns of Saxony and the March of Brandenburg. In these towns Communism had no natural roots and had come, in any case, to be identified in people's minds with foreign oppression. As the news came through it must have seemed as if the Ulbricht regime was finished; the crowds that had at first contented themselves with chanting anti-Communist slogans now turned to storming the Bastille. Thousands of political prisoners were released, and within twenty-four hours of the first downing of tools in the Stalinallee the Russians were faced with nothing less than a national revolt.

As in Hungary, the sequel was tragic in its inevitability. The Russians might have lost confidence in Ulbricht and his German Democratic Republic, but they could scarcely afford to withdraw. Though the Russians might have been willing to sell out in Germany before, now they had to stay put. The revolt in Hungary differed in one respect from the rising three years previously in East Germany: in its greater bitterness and determination. For in East Germany the potentially anti-Communist elements had long had the opportunity to leave the country via the breathing-hole of West Berlin; in Hungary the opposition had remained within the country. And it was also the possibility of escape that rendered the Communist tyranny in East Germany more tolerable.

The 17th of June 1953, in fact, changed very little. Certain concessions were made by the Communist leadership, as indeed some had already been made before the rising broke out, as part of the general slackening of the reins after the death of Stalin. But the position of Ulbricht and his 'Muscovites' was unshakable. Bertolt Brecht addressed an appeal to Ulbricht for greater intellectual freedom in East Germany. The letter was published, but in deliberately mutilated form to give the impression that Brecht endorsed the use of Russian tanks against German workers. For this letter Brecht earned the abuse of his Western colleagues and probably the suspicion and contempt of the official Communists into the bargain. It was evident that East Germany would have to wait long for the benefits of post-Stalinist thaw.

In September 1953 Ernst Reuter died, an event that released a kind of genuine public emotion unfamiliar in an era of massed bands and blaring slogans. As they took leave of him in front of the Schöneberger Town Hall, tens of thousands of Berliners of all classes wept publicly for the first time in their lives. There was a feeling that a great champion of the people had passed away; a Socialist with something of the prophetic stature of Karl Marx or Keir Hardie. But neither a Reuter from outside nor a Bertolt Brecht from within could hope to alter the course which the Russians had decided on for East Germany. The deadly rivalry of the Communist and the anti-Communist Left only served to make the victory of the Right in West Germany more certain.

There is no better illustration of this than the fate of Wolfgang Harich. Harich was one of the most distinguished of the post-war converts to Communism. His theatrical and literary criticism had a brilliance that seemed to belong to the 'twenties rather than to the drab, disillusioned 'forties and 'fifties. At twenty-five he was made professor at the Humboldt University. 'Twentyish, too, was his combination of Marxist orthodoxy with the night life of an Arabian prince: 'I live only for Stalin and for you', he is reported to have told a girl on one occasion. When the thaw set in after Stalin's death, he was one of those who began to discuss with colleagues in Poland and Hungary the chances of a more liberal Marxism. In October 1956, inspired by the Polish example, he started to canvass support for a liberalization of the East German regime and for the removal of Ulbricht. But this revolution too, like Berlin's other revolutions, failed to come off. With a naïveté rivalled only by some of the conspirators of the 20th of July plot, Harich went to Ulbricht and urged him to resign. Ulbricht had his faults: but he was not naïve. Harich was arrested and sentenced to ten years' imprisonment for high treason. But to any reader of Harich's *Testimony*, a document smuggled out to West Berlin, it is evident that no Communist leader could have acted otherwise in these circumstances. Harich was at bottom an Idealist with amazingly little sense of the issues of *Realpolitik* involved. The Communist course in East Germany had to remain 'hard' if the regime was to survive at all.

For this reason no real 'de-Stalinization' ever took place in East Berlin. It was all too clear that the problem of Berlin could only be solved 'at the summit' by the four Allies who were originally responsible for the division of the city. Berlin had become merely a function of the East-West conflict. To some extent, Berlin profited by this conflict. The subsidies of the American and Federal German governments made West Berlin into a flourishing, aggressively modern-looking city where the marks of war-time destruction were either eliminated or obscured by a new wealth of neon lighting. And the Eastern part of the city, too, by virtue of its exposed position was allowed to live above its means. East Berlin enjoyed a considerably higher standard of living than the surrounding Eastern Zone.

The economic recovery of West Berlin, on the other hand, was a genuine affair, and the city became once again an industrial centre of the first importance. The *Interbau* architectural exhibition of the summer of 1957, with buildings by Le Corbusier, Gropius, Niemeyer, and Aalto, carried on that 'internationalism' of which the Berliners had always been inordinately proud. By showing the latest productions of Western enterprise in every field, West Berlin gradually established herself as the West's shop-window to the peoples of Eastern Europe. No visitor from these countries to East Berlin failed to nip over the frontier for a few hours into the mysterious, glittering world of the West from which he had been cut off for so long.

But Berlin's position remained precarious. So long as she continued to live on subsidies from the West a certain unreality in her way of life was inevitable. It was soon possible to distinguish three types of Germans; West Germans, East Germans, and West Berliners. The isolation of West Berlin led to an exaggerated local patriotism. Ernst Reuter did much to encourage this tendency, and it was made worse by the fact that while West Berlin could send members to the Bonn parliament, these were not allowed to vote on account of the continued 'occupation' of Berlin. Willy Brandt, on whom the mantle of Ernst Reuter fell when he was elected Lord Mayor in the autumn of 1957, owed his overwhelming triumph at the polls a year later to this patriotism (Dr. Adenauer, likewise, his discomfiture). But there are obvious dangers here. Brandt himself has argued in the past that certain ministries ought to be transferred from Bonn to Berlin as the *de jure* capital of a united Germany. Yet West Berlin owes its 'freedom' solely to the guarantees given by the Western allies and these are inseparable from the status of an Occupied City. Berlin can not have it both ways: for her, 'Occupation' is the guarantee of 'Freedom'.

It is interesting to speculate which German city would provide Germany with its ideal capital. After 1945, Frankfurt am Main was a much-canvassed city, but it was rejected for Bonn on the personal insistence of Dr. Adenauer. Now Dr. Adenauer is often said to be an anti-Prussian and no friend of Berlin. But his choice of Bonn was intended indirectly to placate the Berliners. He argued that a sleepy Rhine-side provincial town like Bonn could never become the permanent capital of Germany; it would be a reminder to West German members of parliament of the temporary division of their country. In fact, things turned out differently. Bonn soon established itself in the minds of most foreigners—and perhaps of most West

Germans?—as the new capital of Germany. Berlin was in danger of becoming a curiosity, left over from the cold war and the Air Lift, living on its heroic past.

The Soviet initiative of the late autumn of 1958 changed all this. A new Berlin Crisis had come into being. The immediate consequence of renewed Soviet pressure was a resounding defeat for Ulbricht's SED at the polls in West Berlin and a vote of over fifty per cent for the Social Democrats under Willy Brandt. To the Berliners the issue was clear-cut; their city was in danger and they would give their votes to the man most likely to protect their interests. Theirs was a straightforward decision. They preferred the known risks of the *status quo* to the unknown perils of a Free City on the unfortunate model of pre-war Danzig.

Where the outside world might possibly differ was in its estimation of the risks inherent in the *status quo*. Danzig had been, after all, merely a Polish-German problem. But Berlin remained—as we have tried to show in this book—the powerpivot of Europe. Despite the relative decline of Western Europe, the lines of force still met and contended in the city. The situation was fraught with danger for the Great Powers as much as for the Berliners themselves. And it was soon to become evident that the Soviets were less interested in the fate of Berlin (here they differed from their protégés in East Berlin) than in a solution of the German problem as a whole. Berlin was to be used as a weapon to force a settlement. But at this point the matter passed out of the hands of the Berliners. Whether a *modus vivendi* could be found, depended on the goodwill and common sense of those responsible for the continuance of the Cold War. The Berliners have never been great believers in miracles, but resignation and pessimism are equally alien to their nature. Should a miracle occur—and it would have to be a properly certified one; cut, dried, and labelled—they would know how to welcome it and make good use of it. They might even consider that they had deserved it.

INDEX

Adenauer, Konrad, 160, 187
Albert the Bear, 6
Air Lift, 169, 172–3
Armoury, 1, 19, 70
Army, Prussian, rapid expansion of, 18; structure of, 47–8; reformers, 54
Arndt, Ernst Moritz, 54–5, 63, 87
Arnim, Achim von, 50, 60, 63, 81
Arnim, Bettina von, née Brentano, 64, 72, 78
Auden, W. H., 116, 118, 177
Austrians, and Prussians, 11

Bach, Johann Sebastian, 33, 59
Bach, Carl Philipp Emanuel, 33
Bakunin, Mikhail, 76
Bauer, Bruno, 74
Barlach, Ernst, 115
Beaconsfield, Lord, at Congress of Berlin, 90
Becher, Johannes R., 115
Beck, General Ludwig, 54, 177, 142–4, 146
Benn, Gottfried, 107; *Morgue*, 114; attitude to Nazism, 136; 160–3; and Brecht, 177
Berg, Alban, *Wozzeck*, 121
Berlin, Congress of, 91
Berliners, characteristics of, 4–5; colonial origins of, 7; irreligion, 9; attitude to authority, 7–8, 77
Biedermeier, 55, 57–68
Bismarck, Otto von, 6; and *Realpolitik*, 14; 17, 24, 42, 47, 53, 60, 85–91, 96; dismissal, 102; on William II, 103, 164
Blockade, the Berlin, 76, 168–74, 182
Blücher, Field-Marshal, 54, 62
Bonhoeffer, Dietrich, theologian, 137, 138, 144, 145, 146

Borsig, 5, 71, 78, 94
Boyen, General von, 54, 63
Brahm, Otto, 36, 120, 177
Brandenburg, March of, see March of Brandenburg
Brandenburger Tor, 16, 34, 69, 159
Brandt, Willy, 187
Brecht, Bertolt, 44, 108, 115; and Toller, 116; Didactic Plays, 119, 120; *The Punitive Measure*, 126; *Fear and Misery of the Third Reich*, 135; *Mother Courage*, 156; 159; return to Berlin, 175–9; and Workers' Rising, 185–6
Brentano, Clemens von, 50, 60
Bronnen, Arnolt, 115, 119
Brücke, group of painters, 107, 109, 112

Cabinet of Dr Caligari, 107, 119
Captain of Cöpenick see Zuckmayer
Catt, de, 25, 29
Chamisso, Adalbert von, *Undine*, 64; *Peter Schlemihl*, 82
Charlottenburg, 19, 92, 154
Chesterton, G. K., 29, 144
Chodowiecki, Daniel, engraver, 110
Christian German Society, 63, 81, 85
Classicism, and Romanticism, 42–3; Prussian C., 43, 69–71, 110
Clausewitz, Carl von, 42, 54
Clay, General Lucius D., 169
Coleridge, Samuel Taylor, 44, 45
Communism, significance of Berlin to, 76; founding of KPD, 124, 164–6
Corinth, Lovis, painter, 111
Cornelius, Peter, painter, 84

Dadaism, 107, 122–3